*Stories Behind
Popular Songs
and Hymns*

Stories Behind Popular Songs and Hymns

Lindsay L. Terry

Foreword by Jerry Falwell

BAKER BOOK HOUSE
Grand Rapids, Michigan 49516

The following copyright owners have given permission to use their material.

Dedicated
to that marvelous group
of songwriters
who have blessed our hearts
with their great compositions

Contents

Foreword

A few years ago, Lindsay Terry wrote a book titled *Devotionals from Famous Hymn Stories*. This daily devotional guide was so well accepted by the Christian public and so used of God in the lives of literally thousands of people that he has now written another book, *Stories Behind Popular Songs and Hymns*. I have had the opportunity to read the manuscript, and I believe this work will be used of God even beyond the previous book.

Lindsay Terry is a friend. I have known him for many years now and have appreciated his friendship and ministry. He is one of the finest music directors in local church ministry today. He has worked with several great pastors throughout the country and has been used of God in music conferences for years.

Jerry Falwell
Lynchburg, Virginia

Preface

For many years I have delighted in the study of the stories behind our famous hymns and gospel songs. I have found that most of the songs were born out of human suffering. Out of a dark period in the life of one of God's children suddenly there springs forth a ray of light, a sunbeam—a song!

I have gleaned these stories from conversations with those wonderful songwriters, from friends who knew them, and from old periodicals and several books of hymnology. Many of these stories have never been published before this writing.

Although this book is primarily a devotional volume, the contents can be used as sermon illustrations, Sunday school materials, or story backgrounds for children's gatherings.

Other volumes of this nature that I have written have proved to be a spiritual help, and I trust that these additional stories will bring further blessings to the readers. May these stories cause greater glory to come to the Lord Jesus Christ each time you hear one of these wonderful hymns.

Lindsay Terry
Garland, Texas

Acknowledgments

I appreciate the cooperation of the many songwriters who graciously and enthusiastically told the stories behind their beautiful songs. I am also thankful for the people in the copyright offices of numbers of publishing companies, and their kind cooperation.

I am grateful to my wife, Marilyn, who has been a help and an encouragement during this project.

Starr Walker, my secretary, did a commendable job in typing and helping prepare the manuscript.

Finally, I will ever be indebted to the thousands of people who have heard my stories with intense interest as I told them from many platforms. I am thereby encouraged to find more and more information that will enrich our appreciation of Christianity's great heritage of hymns and gospel music.

Introduction

This book is filled with devotional thoughts that tell us of God's love and grace. They were obtained from events in the lives of people who felt moved to express in song the most heartfelt feelings of their spiritual lives.

The effects of music and its contributions to society are phenomenal. An English philosopher said, "Give me the making of the songs of a nation and I care not who makes her laws." Music does affect our lives, whether it be for good or bad.

The need for a book of this type is great. It can be used not only in the home for personal devotionals, but in church meetings, prayer groups, and other gatherings. The history behind each song is warm and unforgettable. But, more than that, one gains a deeper appreciation for the hymn after knowing its origin.

Lindsay Terry has spent many years searching and collecting this information and has done a superb job in revealing it to us. He has for years been a fine musician with a close personal relationship to the Lord and a love for souls, as evidenced in his writings.

This book will increase your love for God and will give you a deeper respect for the great songs of Zion—challenging you and giving you spiritual stepping-stones.

May I recommend this book to you and challenge you to absorb its contents? Great is your loss if this fine work sits stagnant.

Our family will be using it, and I hope yours will be, too

Anita Bryant

19

List of Authors/Composers

List of Song Titles

1

A Frail Giant

Song: *O Happy Day*

Scripture: 2 Timothy 2:1–15

*And the things that thou hast heard of me among many
witnesses, the same commit thou to faithful men, who shall
be able to teach others also.*

How would you like to live in a family with nineteen
brothers and sisters? Such was the home of Philip Doddridge.
Twenty children were born to his parents, an oil merchant and
his saintly Dutch wife. Although Philip was such a frail little
fellow that his parents thought he would not survive, he outlived both of them. They died before he finished grammar
school. Mrs. Doddridge was to have a marked influence in the
life of Philip, her youngest son. She often would draw him to
her knees, as they sat by the fireplace, and tell him stories from
the Bible. These stories were for him a foundation that caused
his life to be useful for the Savior.

It is not known when young Philip came to know Christ as
Savior, but he grew to be a mighty minister of the gospel. He
became the head of an academy where he trained two hundred

young men for the ministry, multiplying his influence many times over. He wrote no less than four hundred hymns and gospel songs, including the familiar "Awake, My Soul."

Philip's frail constitution remained with him into his adult years. He ignored that, it is reported, giving little attention to the care of his body. He was a man of great zeal and compassion and hard work for the Lord. At the age of forty-nine, when in the prime of his work, Doddridge became a victim of the dreaded disease tuberculosis. He decided to go to the dryer climate of Portugal, but his decision came too late. He died in 1751, a few weeks after reaching Lisbon.

Several years after his death, Doddridge's hymns were brought together into one collection and published. One of his most noted songs is "O Happy Day." It is a song of testimony; it speaks of the time when he chose to follow Jesus Christ. As you read this story, have you made that choice? Have you chosen to become a follower of Christ and to be on his side, to be a member of his team? You should, you know.

One report says that after "O Happy Day" had been sung for over a hundred years, an unknown writer added the chorus that we sing today. Following are two stanzas and the chorus of this wonderful gospel song:

> O happy day that fixed my choice,
> On Thee, my Savior and my God!
> Well may this glowing heart rejoice,
> And tell its raptures all abroad.

> Now rest, my long divided heart,
> Fixed on this blissful center, rest;
> Nor ever from my Lord depart,
> With Him of ev'ry good possessed.

> *Chorus*:
> Happy day, happy day,
> When Jesus washed my sins away!
> He taught me how to watch and pray,
> And live rejoicing every day;

Happy day, happy day,
When Jesus washed my sins away.

Reflection: Happy is the man who leaves behind him a work that continues to point men, women, boys, and girls to the Savior long after he has gone to heaven. Does your life really count for Christ today?

2

Is This All for Me?

Song: *Face to Face*
Scripture: Psalm 97
The heavens declare his righteousness, and all the people see his glory.

A pastor, his wife, and Grant Tullar had made their last call on the sick one afternoon in 1898. They hurried to the home of the pastor, wanting to have a bit of supper together before going to the evangelistic meetings that were in progress. Tullar was assisting in those revival services.

In their hurry to get supper on the table, someone failed to fill the jelly dish. There was only a small bite left. The pastor and his wife knew that Tullar was very fond of the jelly, so they both refused it. As the dish was passed to him, he exclaimed, "So this is all for me, is it?" Suddenly, the thought occurred to him that "All for Me" was a good title for a song. The small bit of jelly faded into insignificance as Tullar's mind began to think on this new subject. He placed the jelly dish back on the table and immediately excused himself, went to the piano, and composed a melody and wrote several verses.

Before going to bed that evening, Tullar promised the pastor and his wife that he would revise the work somewhat. He never did, because the next morning the postman brought to him a letter from a lady, Mrs. Frank A. Beck. Enclosed were several poems. After reading the very first poem, he became suddenly aware that it exactly fitted the music that he had written the night before. Not a single word of the poem nor his music needed to be changed. After that, he never used his own words, but decided to use those of Mrs. Beck for the song now titled "Face to Face."

This song has won the hearts of thousands of people around the world because it so wonderfully speaks of our anticipation in seeing Christ one day, face to face, as we now see a friend or loved one. Its words capture the feelings of warmth, brightness, and cheerfulness that expectation imparts:

> Face to face with Christ my Savior,
> Face to face what will it be?
> When with rapture I behold Him,
> Jesus Christ who died for me.
>
> Face to face! O blissful moment!
> Face to face—to see and know;
> Face to face with my Redeemer,
> Jesus Christ Who loves me so.
>
> *Chorus*:
> Face to face I shall behold Him,
> Far beyond the starry sky;
> Face to face in all His glory,
> I shall see Him by and by!

Reflection: A life is never so sweet, the future never so bright, and worldly pleasures never so unattractive than when we, through the light of the Bible, learn to anticipate and live in the blessed hope that one day we will see the Lord—face to face.

3

A Campus Marker

Song: *The Old Rugged Cross*
Scripture: John 19:13–22

And he bearing his cross went forth into a place called the place of a skull, which is called in the Hebrew Golgotha: Where they crucified him, and two others with him, on either side one, and Jesus in the midst.

When polls are taken to determine what are the most popular American hymns, invariably near the top of the list is "The Old Rugged Cross." The popularity of this hymn started during the Billy Sunday campaigns in the earlier parts of this century.

Some claim that the song was written between December 29, 1912, and January 12, 1913. Those who make those claims also say that the song was first sung by the Friends Church at Sturgeon Bay, Michigan. What is certain is that it has been by far the most popular of about three hundred songs written by George Bennard, who lived from 1873 to 1958.

Bennard was born into a very modest family in Youngstown, Ohio. His father passed away in George's teen years, leaving the youth with the tremendous responsibility of helping his mother and his five brothers and sisters. To that end he became a coal miner like his father before him.

The Salvation Army has been a helper of "others" for so many years. This was an attraction to Bennard and his young wife, who joined their ranks and worked with the "Army" for a number of years.

Bennard later felt impressed of the Lord to become an itinerant evangelist, in a time when it was tough to be on the road. He served for years in Canada and some of our northern states. It is also reported that he felt puzzled that others of his hymns did not become as accepted and used by masses of people as "The Old Rugged Cross."

Many hymns are timeless and wear like steel. Such is this great gospel song. One of the great ways to teach Bible doctrines is through songs that are stories set to music. A classic example is "The Old Rugged Cross." The Bible says that we are to use such songs in our churches to reach and disciple other Christians: "Let the word of Christ dwell in you richly in all wisdom; teaching and admonishing one another in psalms and hymns and spiritual songs, singing with grace in your hearts to the Lord" (Col. 3:16).

The young people of Albion College, a Methodist school in Albion, Michigan, are used to a certain marker on their campus. And you and I would be quite taken by this remembrance, put there by the Michigan Historical Commission to honor the man who wrote:

> On a hill far away stood an old rugged cross,
> The emblem of suff'ring and shame;
> And I love that old cross where the dearest and best
> For a world of lost sinners was slain.
>
> *Chorus*:
> So I'll cherish the old rugged cross,
> Till my trophies at last I lay down;
> I will cling to the old rugged cross,
> And exchange it some day for a crown.

Reflection: How marvelous that Christ's cross of shame became to you and me a badge of honor, a promise of the kingdom.

4

An Almshouse
Launching Pad

Song: *I Gave My Life for Thee*
Scripture: John 10:1–18
No man taketh it from me, but I lay it down of myself. I have power to lay it down, and I have power to take it again. This commandment have I received of my Father.

Wherever in the world the Christian message has gone, women have been lifted from bondage and suppression and have been placed in a higher position. Though some men do not like to admit it, some of the greatest contributions to humanity and Christendom have been made by the fairer sex. Elizabeth Barrett Browning had this to say in defense of womankind:

> Not SHE with traitorous kiss her Savior stung;
> Not SHE denied Him with unholy tongue;
> She, while apostles shrank, could danger brave,
> Last at His cross and earliest at His grave.

Frances Ridley Havergal (1836–1879) is one of those women whose contributions to the spreading of the Christian message is deemed very great indeed! Though her body was sickly, her life radiated with the love of her Savior. She was brought up in the home of a preacher of the gospel, which contributed much to her fine character. She began her poetic ventures at the age of seven and later studied music and became an accomplished singer and pianist. As an adult, though mainly confined to a wheelchair, Miss Havergal remained cheerful and was a blessing to all those with whom she came in contact. (You can find out more about her life in another story of mine, which appeared in my previous book, *Devotionals from Famous Hymn Stories*.)

Fifteen years after the writing of "I Gave My Life for Thee," Miss Havergal related that it nearly went into the fire instead of around the world. Written in 1859, when she was a young girl, it was the first thing she wrote that could be called a hymn. She did not, it seems, fully realize what she was writing about. She felt that she was following far off, always doubting and fearing. At that time her faith seemed to be very weak and lacked the real conviction that Christ wants his followers to have. Scribbling the words of the hymn on the back of a circular, she read them over and then thought that it was not even poetry. She decided she would not even write them out clearly and reached out her hand to put the paper in the fire, but a sudden impulse made her draw it back. She crumpled it and put it in her pocket.

A few days later she visited an old friend in the almshouse. As the poor lady began talking about her love for the Savior, Miss Havergal thought of the verses she had written and pulled them out of her pocket and began to read them aloud. The friend was so delighted with the poem that Miss Havergal took further pains to write them out. From that point they have made their way around the world and have been a blessing to millions.

A finer song of consecration cannot be found. P. P. Bliss, the composer of "Hold the Fort" and "Let the Lower Lights Be Burning," wrote a melody for the lyrics. Miss Havergal's father, William, wrote the music to which it was first sung, but Bliss's tune has become more popular in America.

I gave My life for thee,
My precious blood I shed,
That thou might'st ransomed be,
And quickened from the dead;

I gave, I gave My life for thee,
What hast thou given for Me?
I gave, I gave My life for thee,
What hast thou given for Me?

Reflection: God withholds nothing from us, and he requires of his children the same attitude of bountiful giving. It is only as we give to him that our coffers become full, running over with blessings.

5

And We Do Remember Him

Song: *When They Ring the Golden Bells*
Scripture: 1 Corinthians 13
Though I speak with the tongues of men and of angels, and have not charity, I am become as sounding brass, or a tinkling cymbal.

As we go along from day to day, we meet many people who can do at least one thing well. Few and scattered, though, are those versatile individuals who can do many things masterfully.

One such person was Daniel A. DeMarbelle, later known as Dion DeMarbelle. Born in France on July 4, 1818, he joined himself to a whaling ship while quite young and roamed the Arctic Ocean for several of his early years. In 1847, he joined the United States Navy and fought in the Mexican War. The next years were probably even more exciting, because that was when DeMarbelle really embarked upon his varied career.

Immediately after the Mexican War, he toured the country with an opera company as an actor and singer. When James A. Bailey, of "Barnum and Bailey" fame, first organized his circus,

DeMarbelle was one of the performers. He later organized his own show but was forced to close it down when fire destroyed his tents in Canada. After this he turned to helping Colonel William Cody ("Buffalo Bill") establish his "Wild West" show.

It has been reported that DeMarbelle could speak extemporaneously on any subject, displaying an unusual amount of eloquence and oratory. To add to this, he was a sleight-of-hand artist, a poet, and a composer of popular ballads. He sang regularly in a Methodist church choir. But, like many men who have achieved fame and fortune, he was not satisfied with his contribution to mankind. He wanted to leave something lasting, so he wrote the words and music to this now-familiar song:

> There's a land beyond the river
> That we call the sweet forever
> And we only reach that shore by faith's decree;
> One by one we'll gain the portals,
> There to dwell with the immortals,
> When they ring the golden bells for you and me.
>
> *Chorus*:
> Don't you hear the bells now ringing,
> Don't you hear the angels singing?
> 'Tis the glory hallelujah, jubilee,
> In that far off, sweet forever,
> Just beyond the shining river,
> When they ring those golden bells for you and me.

DeMarbelle's last years were spent in utter poverty. Only the generosity of his neighbors kept him alive. Because he had served as a musician in the federal army in the Civil War, he was buried in Soldier's Reserve at Bluff City Cemetery near Elgin, Illinois, by the G.A.R. The marker at his grave reads, "Drum Major D. A. DeMarbelle, 6 Mich. Inf." Thus ended the colorful career of a man remembered primarily as the author of a gospel song that everybody loves, "When They Ring the Golden Bells for You and Me."

Only if we, like Daniel DeMarbelle, recognize that our days are numbered do we come face to face with the desire to depart this life only after making some lasting contribution to mankind. Not one person in his right mind wants to have it said about him in the end that he lived only for himself.

Reflection: God has placed within your breast an intrinsic desire for accomplishment that will make life better for others, though all too often this is choked by the satanic monster called "selfishness." You can be assured that you have begun to grow as a Christian when you can say with meaning and sincerity that you want "less of self and more of Thee."

6

An Old Hymn
Inspires a New Song

Song: *Sweet Beulah Land*
Scripture: John 14:1–11
*And if I go and prepare a place for you, I will come again,
and receive you unto myself; that where I am, there ye may
be also.*

Occasionally a single song brings acclaim and recognition to its composer, although the songwriter might have written several others. Such was the case with Squire Parsons and his most famous song, "Sweet Beulah Land," which was named "song of the year" in 1981 by The Singing News Fan Awards.

Parsons was born in Newton, West Virginia, in 1948, into the home of Christian parents. His father was the songleader and choir director of the local church, and the older Parsons figures prominently in the writing of his son's song. Squire began his writing ventures at age twenty. He studied music at a West Virginia college and later taught music as a band and choir director at Hannan High School near Point Pleasant, West Virginia.

When Squire was only nine, during a morning service in the

small church in Newton where Squire's father was songleader, the congregation was led in the old hymn, "Is Not This the Land of Beulah?" Squire reports that his dad's face seemed to glow as he led the song. The whole congregation seemed swept up into the wonderful prospect of the eternal land about which they were singing. The picture remained in the mind of young Parsons, and he remembers thinking, *Dad is looking into Beulah Land.*

He also reports: "One morning, years later, as I drove to my teaching job, my mind drifted back to the service in our little church. I was humming the old song. As I topped one of the beautiful West Virginia mountains, I faced a brilliant sun in all its glory. All of a sudden my mind went back to the scene in our little church when I was only nine." Parsons remembers that he suddenly began to sing, this time not the old hymn, but the chorus of the song now known as "Sweet Beulah Land":

> I'm kind of homesick for a country
> To which I've never been before.
> No sad good-byes will there be spoken
> And time won't matter any more.
>
> I'm looking now across the river
> To where my faith shall end in sight.
> There's just a few more days to labor
> Then I will take my heav'nly flight.
>
> *Chorus*:
> Beulah Land, I'm longing for you
> And some day on thee I'll stand.
> There my home shall be eternal,
> Beulah Land, Sweet Beulah Land.

Its songwriter adds: "I traveled on to the school. It was early. The students had not yet arrived. I wrote a verse to go with the chorus that had just been born. Five years went by before I wrote a second verse and recorded the song. That launched me into the ministry of a traveling gospel singer and songwriter."

Squire Parsons now crisscrosses our nation, singing his songs and reminding all of us of the beautiful prospect of "Sweet Beulah Land."

Reflection: The anticipation of an eternal heavenly home will make our lives on earth all the more wonderful.

7

A Pioneer Leaves
a Song

Song: *The Eastern Gate*

Scripture: Psalm 30

For his anger endureth but a moment; in his favour is life: weeping may endure for a night, but joy cometh in the morning.

The small town of Kirksville, Missouri, was the birthplace of the Reverend I. G. Martin, one of the great songwriters of years gone by. Martin was born on April 18, 1862, and became a Christian at a very early age, although sometime after his conversion he began to drift away from his commitment to the Lord.

After receiving his college training, Martin began a career as a teacher. This vocation was short-lived, however, and young Martin turned his attention to the stage, where he performed as an actor and singer. This led him further away from his profession of Christ as Savior.

As the years went by, one day he found himself in a revival service in Milwaukee, Wisconsin, where services were led by a Methodist evangelist named Tillotsen. P. P. Bilhorn was the singer and songleader for those meetings. After hearing the preaching and singing of those revivalists, Martin rededicated his life to Christ and determined to serve the Lord again. He later entered the ministry as an evangelistic singer.

Martin soon began to preach as well as sing. His travels carried him to many places in our nation where he spoke and sang in churches and camp meetings. During these years of ministry, he began to write songs that seemingly flowed eloquently from his soul.

In the early years of The Church of The Nazarene, Martin was appointed by Dr. Bresee as superintendent of the eastern district, which consisted of the territory east of the Rocky Mountains. For six years he served the First Nazarene Church in Chicago and later moved to Malden, Massachusetts.

Martin lived for nearly a century. He passed away in August 1957. Haldor Lillenas, who knew him for a portion of the fifty or more years that he preached the gospel, said, "He was indeed one of the staunch pioneers of our church. He lived long and well, loved his Lord fervently, served his church faithfully and was a devoted husband and father."

Millions of Christians are glad that before he departed this life, I. G. Martin wrote a beautiful song about heaven. And so, happily we sing "The Eastern Gate":

> I will meet you in the morning,
> Just inside the Eastern Gate,
> Then be ready, faithful pilgrim,
> Lest with you it be too late.
>
> O, the joy of that glad meeting
> With the saints who for us wait,
> What a blessed, happy meeting,
> Just inside the Eastern Gate.
>
> *Chorus*:
> I will meet you in the morning,
> I will meet you in the morning,
> Just inside the Eastern Gate over there;

I will meet you in the morning,
I will meet you in the morning,
I will meet you in the morning over there.

This wonderful song has experienced a revival in popularity in recent years. It is truly a favorite of thousands of Christians.

Reflection: When our loved ones are taken into the arms of God himself, joy and peace unspeakable should flood our very souls.

8

A Rare Christmas Day

Song: *His Name Is Wonderful*
Scripture: Philippians 2:1–11
Wherefore God also hath highly exalted him, and given him a name which is above every name.

The angel's halo was a little crooked and the shepherds had their pants rolled up under their bathrobes, but something wonderful was about to take place. A beautiful song was soon to be born.

Audrey Mieir, who wrote that song, tells us what happened on that day, one of those rare Christmases that came on Sunday:

> We wanted to do something special in our little church, Bethel Union Church in Duarte, California. The pastor was my brother-in-law. We were using the young people in a Christmas presentation. Mary was a teenage girl and the angels were young boys. The baby was a doll.
>
> The whole place smelled of pine boughs, which we used to decorate the church. The atmosphere was charged. I so often have thought that I could hear the rustling of angels' wings. It seemed that the whole room was filled with the presence of the angels of God.

I looked down at the little children and they were sitting there with open mouths, thinking, as they listened to the soft organ music. I looked around at the older people and they were wiping tears away, remembering many other Christmases gone by.

The pastor stood up and slowly lifted his hands toward heaven and said, "His name is Wonderful!" Those words electrified me. I immediately began writing in the back of my Bible. As I wrote I was thinking that God has something he wants said. I wrote a simple chorus and I sang it that night for the young people around the piano. They sang it immediately. It wasn't hard for them to learn. I never dreamed that it would go any further, but it has traveled around the world in many languages.

Audrey Mieir was born in Pennsylvania in 1916. She began her songwriting career at age sixteen. How thankful we should be that God chose to use her talents to praise him with these simple but powerful words:

> His name is Wonderful,
> His name is Wonderful,
> His name is Wonderful,
> Jesus, my Lord.
> He is the mighty King,
> Master of everything,
> His name is Wonderful,
> Jesus, my Lord.
> He's the great Shepherd,
> The Rock of all ages,
> Almighty God is He;
> Bow down before Him,
> Love and adore Him,
> His name is Wonderful,
> Jesus, my Lord.

Reflection: Is the name of Jesus wonderful to you today and every day? Sing a song of praise and you will feel closer to him. You, too, will experience that "his name is Wonderful."

9

One Last Song

Song: *His Name Is Wonderful*

Scripture: 2 Corinthians 5:1–15

(For we walk by faith, not by sight:) We are confident, I say, and willing rather to be absent from the body, and to be present with the Lord.

One of the great experiences in Audrey Mieir's interesting and useful life happened at the Christian Booksellers Convention in Philadelphia in 1970. This acclaimed songwriter didn't want to be there but had agreed to be present in her publisher's booth to help sell the music. She remembers that day well:

> I really was just complaining to myself. I was all ready for the day's activity.
>
> I looked outside through the door. It was about five minutes until opening time. Everyone who gets in is supposed to have proper identification. I saw this little old lady with a hat and gloves on, and she was very nervous. I could tell instinctively that she was not a bookstore owner and that she was out of place in this group. The guard took down the rope, blocking the way, and she looked right at me and started coming toward

me. I had the feeling that something very special was going to happen.

She came and stood before me and pushed her hat up and said: "Audrey Mieir, I don't own a bookstore." I wanted to hug her right then because I just knew. . . .

She said, "When I heard that you were going to be here I asked if I could come in for just one minute. I have something I want to tell you. I'm almost eighty. My husband and I sang together all of the years of our lives. Daddy had a beautiful tenor voice. I sang the melody and he always sang the tenor. Through our young days we always sang in beautiful and large places. As the years came and went, our voices began to grow old. Finally, there was nothing left but convalescent homes and hospitals. But we gladly went anywhere we could, because we loved Jesus so much.

"One day my husband, who was a tall, strong man having never had a sick day in his life, doubled up with an extreme pain. It frightened me to death because I could never imagine him being sick.

"We rushed him to the hospital and they put him in for exploratory surgery. They sent me home and said it would be a while before they could tell me what was really wrong. I sat there in that apartment looking at the walls, and it seemed like my whole world was crumbling in! Soon came the phone call, 'Come to the hospital! Your husband is calling for you.' I took a taxi, went to the hospital, and walked to the door of the room. I almost felt as though I was going to faint. I didn't think I could stand to see him in that condition. I opened the door and looked in and saw him on the bed. He turned toward me, opened his eyes and his arms and said, 'Mama come here.' I looked around to be sure no one was looking. He said, 'Mama, I called you in so that we could sing one more song together.' I said, 'Sing, at this time?' He answered, 'Yes, let's sing our favorite song, *His Name Is Wonderful*. Can you get the pitch?' He held onto my hand and I closed my eyes and I got the pitch and started to sing. All of a sudden I heard this beautiful tenor voice—it was beautiful and clear.

"We came to the words, 'Bow down before Him,' and all of a sudden I was singing . . . alone. I went on and finished the song. I looked down. He had gone home to be with Jesus."

And then she said, "I just wanted to thank you for writing

that beautiful song that took Dad home to heaven." Then she reached down and took my face in her hands.

I was just paralyzed. All of a sudden she was gone. I then went behind a curtain and thanked God for allowing me to write a song that would take someone to heaven.

Reflection: We must all live every day so that the precious things of God are alive in us. These moments that we spend here, each day, will also usher us into the presence of the Lord. May it be a happy homecoming as we "bow down before Him."

10

A Rush Act on the Printer

Song: *Take My Hand, Precious Lord*
Scripture: Psalm 37:1–8
Delight thyself also in the LORD; and he shall give thee the desires of thine heart. Commit thy way unto the LORD; trust also in him; and he shall bring it to pass.

In 1899, little notice was taken of a baby boy born in Villa Rica, Georgia, a small town about forty miles from Atlanta. But this baby was to become a blues entertainer called "Georgia Tom" and later, after his commitment to Christ, a leader in the field of gospel music. Thomas A. Dorsey wrote about three hundred songs and directed choirs for more than fifty years, most of that time at the Pilgrim Baptist Church in Chicago.

In about 1977 Thomas Dorsey told me the following story, which happened in 1932:

My wife, Nettie, was about to bear our first child. I was called to St. Louis to sing in a revival. I wondered if I should go, because of my wife's condition. She persuaded me that I should go ahead.

I asked a friend to go with me. When we were a good way out of town, I remembered that I left my music case at home. I knew that I must have my music, so I drove back to get it. At that point my friend decided that he would not make the trip with me after all. So I drove to St. Louis alone.

During the first night of the meetings, a lad brought a telegram to me while I was still on the platform. It was horrible news. It was a message that my wife had died giving birth to our son. I rushed to a phone while the people were still singing, and I found that the message was true. Mr. Gus Evans drove me back to Chicago that night.

When I arrived, I found that the wonderful baby boy was seemingly fine, and yet that night he died also. I buried my wife and son in the same casket.

During the next few days, I became so despondent. I was filled with grief. I had thoughts of going back to the world's music, and yet I knew that God had taken me out of all of that.

I went over to Madame Malone's College to see a good friend, Professor Frye. We walked around the campus for a while and then went into one of the music rooms. I sat down at a piano and began to improvise on the keyboard. Suddenly I found myself playing a particular melody that I hadn't played before. I began to say, "Blessed Lord, Blessed Lord." My friend walked over to me and said, "Why don't you make that 'Precious Lord'?" I began to sing:

> Precious Lord, take my hand,
> Lead me on, help me stand,
> I am tired, I am weak, I am worn.
> Through the storm, through the night,
> Lead me on to the light.
> Take my hand, precious Lord,
> Lead me home.

We used the song before it was published, and so many people wanted a copy of it that we put a rush act on the printer and got the song out. And it has been going ever since.

Thomas Dorsey's song has been translated into thirty-two languages in many countries around the world.

Reflection: The Lord will never leave us comfortless nor forsake us. When we despair in the darkness of life's afflictions, we need only reach out and he will be there to answer every need and bring us into the warm glow of his light.

11

A Symbol of Christian Liberty

Song: *Statue of Liberty*
Scripture: Col. 1:19–27
. . . having made peace through the blood of his cross, by him to reconcile all things unto himself. . . .

The coveted Dove Award was won in 1974 by a very moving, thought-provoking song, written by Neil Enloe. Then thirty-six, this singer/songwriter from Wood River, Illinois, had been raised in a Christian home and had started his music writing career at age eighteen, about the time he entered Central Bible College. Enloe had become a Christian just four years earlier.

The song was born out of a sense of allegiance to his Lord and to his country. Enloe tells its story:

I was a member of a singing group called the Couriers, based in Harrisburg, Pennsylvania. It was in the early 1970s. We were scheduled to sing for a boat ride sponsored by a large group of Christian young people from New York and New

Jersey. They had rented a cruise boat for an evening, and we were to be the musical guests.

There were 2400 people on the boat, with an auditorium that seated only 400. We had to sing six concerts in order for them all to attend during the evening. We had only a five-minute break between the concerts.

During one of the breaks, a member of the group and I went out on deck and were watching the sights along the shore. By this time it was dark. As I stood leaning on the ship's rail with my back to the shore, I saw kids looking excitedly at something and at the same time they began to Ooo and Ahhh. I turned and saw the Statue of Liberty in all her glory, ablaze with lights.

Because I was raised in the Midwest, everything patriotic in me suddenly rose to the surface. I had never seen it so closely before. It was so very, very close. In my own mind and heart, I realized, anew and afresh, the liberty I have as an American citizen.

I turned to the fellow with me and I said, "There must be a counterpart to my American freedom—liberty in Christ. There is surely a monument to this liberty!" I thought, *There is no greater symbol to Christian liberty than the cross!*

I turned to my friend and said, "There should be a song somewhere in this."

After three months of writing and rewriting, Neil Enloe gave to the world his award-winning song, "Statue of Liberty":

> In New York harbor stands a lady,
> With a torch raised to the sky;
> And all who see her know she stands for
> Liberty for you and me.
> I'm so proud to be called an American,
> To be named with the brave and the free;
> I will honor our flag and our trust in God,
> And the Statue of Liberty.
>
> On lonely Golgotha stood a cross,
> With my Lord raised to the sky;
> And all who kneel there live forever

As all the saved can testify.
I'm so glad to be called a Christian,
To be named with the ransomed and whole;
As the statue liberates the citizen,
So the cross liberates the soul.

O the cross is my Statue of Liberty.
It was there that my soul was set free;
Unashamed I'll proclaim that a rugged cross
Is my Statue of Liberty.

Reflection: Christ, and he alone, is our Rescuer, for he left his majestic position and condescended to provide freedom and salvation for lowly human beings through the power of God's love. He is to enjoy a place of exaltation in our hearts, for he is King of kings and Lord of lords.

12

A Sudden Calm
and Peaceful Rest

Song: *Because He Lives*
Scripture: John 14:12–20
Yet a little while, and the world seeth me no more; but ye see me: because I live, ye shall live also.

Two of the most talented songwriters of our time, or of any age, are Bill and Gloria Gaither. What a multitude of marvelous songs have come from their hearts and their dedicated minds! Both have a marvelous Christian heritage that plays such a dominant role in their spiritual lives and daily activities.

Almost since their marriage in the early sixties, the Gaithers, two-thirds of The Bill Gaither Trio, have touched the lives of millions around the world. Together they have written more than five hundred published songs, many of which are favorites throughout Christendom.

In the late 1960s, while expecting their third child, the Gaithers were going through a rather traumatic time in their lives. Bill was recovering his strength from a bout with mononucleosis. They, along with their church, were the objects of accusation and belittlement. Gloria was experiencing a time of torment, including fear of the future and of bringing children into such a crazy, mixed-up world.

As Gloria sat alone in a darkened living room, tormented, fearful, and thoughtful, the Lord knew her need and suddenly sent to her a calm and peaceful rest. The panic left and was replaced by a peace that surpasses all understanding—an assurance that the future would be fine, left in God's hands.

The presence of the Holy Spirit was particularly precious as the Gaithers remembered that his strength and power were at their disposal. The power of the resurrection of Christ seemed to affirm itself in their lives once again. Gloria remembers the realization that "it was LIFE conquering death in the regularity of my day." The joy seemed to overcome and take precedent over frightening human circumstances.

In her book, *Fully Alive,* Gloria relates the following story that took place shortly after that marvelous experience:

> One day in the late fall, we had some men come to pave the parking lot behind our office. They brought load after load of coarse rocks, pea gravel and sand. They brought huge heavy rollers and smashed all of that down. Again and again they rolled it. Finally came the steaming truckloads of molten asphalt to be poured atop the gravel, then rolled again and again until it was smooth and hard and "permanent."
>
> Very early the next spring, Bill's dad came into the office one morning, and stood around on first one foot then the other, grinning as he does when there's something special on his mind.
>
> "Come out here," he finally said to Bill and me. We followed him out the back door onto the shining new pavement. Right in the middle of it he stopped and pointed, "Look, there."
>
> Up through the sand, up through the gravel, up through the rocks, up from the darkness and through the thick layer of asphalt had pushed a green shoot. It wasn't tough, it wasn't sharp, it wasn't strong. Any child could have plucked it up with nearly no effort at all. *But it was alive!* And there it stood, bright green in the sunlight, boasting to the world of its photosynthetic miracle: *life wins!*
>
> There wasn't much to say. We just smiled our message of

reassurance at each other; but I couldn't help thinking of the song we had just written after our own personal bout with darkness:

> God sent His Son; they called Him Jesus.
> He came to love, heal and forgive.
> He bled and died to buy my pardon;
> An empty grave is there to prove
> MY SAVIOR LIVES.
>
> How sweet to hold our newborn baby,
> And feel the pride and joy he gives;
> But greater still the calm assurance:
> Our child can face uncertain days
> BECAUSE HE LIVES.
>
> Because He lives
> I can face tomorrow!
> Because He lives
> All fear is gone!
> Because I know
> He holds the future,
> And life is worth the living
> JUST BECAUSE HE LIVES!

Reflection: The awareness and the assurance of the Savior's resurrection gives strength to overcome the frightening obstacles of life—because he lives every day in my heart.

13

Cleansed and Made New

Song: *I'm Not What I Want to Be*

Scripture: Ephesians 2:1–10

But God, who is rich in mercy, for his great love wherewith he loved us, Even when we were dead in sins, hath quickened us together with Christ, (by grace ye are saved).

As with all of us, past events in the lives of Bill and Gloria Gather have had a profound effect on their present actions. One of their most widely known songs is a personal testimony, a song that grew out of their commitment to Christ. It is a testimony of what happens when an individual is freed from the sadness and despair that people without Christ so often feel. The story deals with early events in Gloria's life and how she gained freedom and joy in Christ.

Gloria was raised in a marvelous Christian home, a preacher's home, in a small rural community in Michigan. How fortunate for a little girl to grow up in a human family where she is, first of all, loved—and then drawn personally into the problems and triumphs, defeats and victories, and joys and sorrows of that home.

She learned early on what personal faith in Christ is all

about and tells of vivid memories of family worship. As with most small children, there were both spurts of interest and periods of boredom during these family times of devotions. Yet, they were the times when problems were met and solved by searching the Word of God and through praying.

The children in Gloria's home learned the wonders and intrigue of nature as they roamed the nearby Michigan woods, where they gained an abiding respect and admiration for the animals and their habitat. Consider a meaningful story that seems to be answered in a powerful song. Here is the story in Gloria's words, as told in *Fully Alive!*

> My parents were pastors of a small church in a tiny Michigan farm community. I was practically born in church and was intimate with the truth of the Scriptures almost from the beginning. . . . I developed an understanding of right and wrong very early. . . . I understood the plan of salvation, and the responsibility of the individual for making a choice of direction in life.
>
> It was a warm midsummer day in 1946 that all these experiences brought me to a place of confrontation with myself. In spite of my happy childhood, I became more and more aware of conflict inside myself. I felt unhappy and troubled. More and more I found myself resenting my sister and arguing with her over any little thing. I went through the motions of being a part of the family, but felt a gap growing between what I was on the inside and what I tried to pretend on the outside.
>
> That day I had a particularly ugly argument with my sister. Although I controlled my reaction to her, my little heart was filled with hatred and bitterness. I slammed out the back door of our old farmhouse and threw myself down on the grass in the backyard. I was seething with anger and the desire to hurt and strike out.
>
> In the grass I saw a small long-legged spider. I had played with "granddaddy longlegs" many times, and I knew them to be harmless, defenseless creatures, but this one became the object of my hateful attitude. Slowly, one by one, I began to pull off its legs, enjoying its misery and my power.
>
> Each leg I amputated left the spider more vulnerable. Finally, only the round, buttonlike body was left. I dropped the spider in the grass, and watched the muscle inside that little, round

body struggle. No legs, but the "granddaddy longlegs" wasn't dead. Spitefully, I rose to my feet, turned my back on it, and walked into the house.

I am almost hesitant to tell this story, knowing that some may belittle the importance of a child's experience and smile at an act that may not seem so serious. But I take the risk in order to illustrate a principle of life: *sin always has its root in the heart.* It is our motive that is so important. Sometimes we tend to take lightly the transgressions and confessions of children. But my sin that day, small as it may seem to me now as an adult, was just as real as any other act of rebellion and violence against the sacredness of life.

As I went through the day, the guilt of what I had done weighed heavily on my mind. Finally, some time later, I returned to the spot in the yard to try to find the little creature and, at least, to put it out of its misery, but I couldn't find it. So I learned a second principle of life: *once a law of God has been broken, we can never on our own put things back the way they were.* Like Humpty Dumpty, the purity of innocence, once shattered, can never quite, by our own efforts at reform, be restored.

All through that day I went around like half a person, but no one seemed to notice. Clocks went on ticking, the family routine continued as usual, the sun set in the west, but for me something had died.

How I dreaded family worship that night! And just as I feared, it went right on as usual. They accepted me as they always had, as a loved and important member of our family and God's. I endured the Scripture reading, and quickly prayed a routine prayer so that the turn could pass to my sister and mother. But by the time my father began to pray, I was feeling such conviction that I couldn't let the worship go on.

I can still see the scene in the living room that night with the whole family kneeling in prayer. Finally, I couldn't fight back the tears anymore. I crawled across to where my mother was kneeling and whispered, "I have to pray." I had just finished praying, but she didn't question me for a moment. She understood immediately what I meant and stopped my dad in the middle of his sentence. He and my sister came to where I was and put their arms around me as I began to sob out my need for forgiveness. Like the child I was, I simply confessed everything I could think of that stood between me and a clear relationship with them and God and asked Jesus to take control of my life and make me new again. He did.

The heaviness of the guilt I had felt lifted, and I knew I would soar again. I was a child again, all clean and new. I had been "born" again.

In the next moments there was—how shall I say?—a "flood of caring" for others. I guess I would have to call it a shower of love. I wanted to hug the whole world. I began to talk to my new Master about everyone I knew, lifting their needs and hurts and heartaches to Him, making myself available for Him to use to help answer my own prayers. I just felt *loved* and free to take the risk of loving.

No wonder people have such a hard time finding a name for it! Conversion—"being saved," "being transformed," "being redeemed." I guess I'd just have to call it finding out what it really means to be loved with God's love, the power that shaped the worlds from nothingness. When that power touches a mere human being, something happens! Creation all over again! Yes, I'd been touched by LOVE!

As life-changing and unforgettable as that initial personal encounter with Christ was for me, it was only the beginning of a long process of learning and growth. Just as I was a simple child at the time, I was also a fledgling in the things of the Spirit. There would be many new demands for commitment along my path; I would come to know failure and doubt. But there was no denying that God had invaded my life, and I would never be the same. I chose to follow Him wherever that might lead.[1]

Years later, Gloria found herself looking back to that experience, thanking the Lord for the progress he had allowed her to make in her Christian life, and she penned the lyrics to a beautiful song, "I'm Not What I Want to Be, But Thank God I'm Not What I Was." Her husband, Bill, and Gary Paxton set the poem to music. And so we have:

> When I started out on my journey,
> I had such a long way to go,
> It was just a start when I gave Him my heart.

1. From *Fully Alive* by Gloria Gaither (Nashville: Thomas Nelson, 1984), pp. 20–25.

There was such a lot I needed to know.
Now I look back over my shoulder,
I can see that I've come a long way.
Oh, I'm not what I want to be,
But thank God I'm not what I was.

I'm learning to be happy, just growing,
For struggle is part of life.
Believing always comes before knowing,
And victory comes after the strife.
So, I'm not what I want to be,
I'm not what I'm going to be,
But thank God I'm not what I was.

Reflection: Happy indeed is the person who is clean before the Lord who knew no sin. To be justified in his sight brings joy beyond description.

14

Standing with the Family

Song: *The Family of God*
Scripture: 1 John 4:7–21
Beloved, if God so loved us, we ought also to love one another.

For nearly thirty years, Bill and Gloria Gaither have influenced the singing of Christians around the world. One major tool has been the recording of forty-five albums of songs. Indications of their influence and acceptance have been two Grammy Awards and dozens of Dove Awards. The Gospel Music Association named them "songwriter of the year" nine times. Gloria has written ten books and Bill and Gloria have co-written ten major musicals. Their music-publishing companies have circulated their music and books for many years.

God has given only a few people in this world an ability to compose song after song that combine beautiful lyrics and infectious, singable melodies. Such are the Gaithers. They seem to be always open to the leading of the Holy Spirit in the writing of a song. The creative individuals who write our songs influence our lives more than we can ever imagine.

One of the Gaithers' most meaningful and widely used songs was written in 1970. It was born out of hardship and trial, as are many of the most lasting of our beloved hymns and gospel songs.

The Gaithers are faithful members of a local church in Alexandria, Indiana, and the church body is very dear to them. A young family in their congregation, Ron and Darlene Garner and their three children, was used to inspire the writing of the Gaithers' song "The Family of God," according to Gloria Gaither in her book *Because He Lives* ([Old Tappan, N.J., Revell, 1988] pp. 123-29):

It was the Saturday after Good Friday that Ron went in for work at the garage where he was serving as a mechanic. He was working alone that day because he was making up time that he had taken off the previous Thursday to take his little daughter for some tests prior to some anticipated heart surgery. With the operation coming up, he knew they would need the money for hospital and doctor bills. While Ron was working with combustible material, there was an explosion. He managed to crash his way through the large double doors before the building blew apart and went up in flames, but he was severely burned over most of his body.

The news from the emergency ward in Muncie was indeed pessimistic: Ron was alive but was not expected to make it through the night. It was only minutes before a chain of telephone calls alerted the Family of God, and the whole church began to pray for Ron. All day long they prayed. Little groups, bigger groups, in homes, at the church, over the phone—all over town the people who were related to Ron and Darlene because of Jesus prayed. By evening the word came that, although the doctors gave no hope, Ron was still alive. They couldn't understand how he was holding on, but they said that, now that he had lived eight hours, possibly, if he could make it until morning, there was a chance—just a chance.

The Family kept on praying. Old folks prayed alone in their rooms. Children prayed in simple faith. Women prayed as they went about the tasks of caring for their families. Men prayed together in basements and over store counters and in automobiles. The church building was kept open, and lights burned all through the night as a steady stream of folks who cared and loved came to talk to Jesus about this young father who was "bone of their bone and flesh of their flesh."

The sun streamed in the windows that Easter morning on a sanctuary filled with the most weary, bleary-eyed congregation you've ever seen. There were very few Easter bonnets or bright new outfits. We were just there, drawn together closer than we had ever been before by the reality we had been sharing—that when one part of the Body suffers, we all suffer with it.

Nobody felt much like celebrating. There was hurt and there was pain in the Body, and that pain had drawn the attention of every other member. About twenty minutes into the service, the pastor came in with a report from the hospital. Although he had gone without sleep to be with the Garner family through the long hours, there was sunshine in his eyes. "Ron has outlived the deadline. The doctors say he has a chance. They are going to begin treatment."

For the Body of Christ, that news was better than eight hours of sleep and a good breakfast. New life was infused into us all. Tears of praise and joy began to flow, and our hope and gratitude poured itself into the glorious songs of Easter. "Jesus lives, and because He lives, we too shall live!"

Those songs that day were for us songs of commitment, too. We knew that the long, hard days for Ron and Darlene and the children had only just begun. With the words of victory we pledged ourselves to the reality of what would lie ahead: help with the children, many long trips to the hospital, pints of blood for transfusions, money for the astronomic hospital bills, meals to be taken to the family who would be too tired to cook, long months of support while the slow skin grafting and healing process went on. We knew what it would mean, and in our celebration we pledged ourselves to whatever it would take to make that injured part of the Body whole and well again.

On our way home from church that morning we [Bill and I] were so full of the beauty of it all that we could hardly speak. Finally, we said to each other what we had come to realize through all this: "They'd do that for us, too!" It was almost too grand to realize, but it was true! We aren't very model church members. The function we fill in the Body of Christ takes us away from a lot of the activities of our congregation. We're never available on Fridays and Saturdays. We get in early on Sunday mornings in time to get our children ready and to their Sunday school and church, but we can't be counted on to teach a class with a schedule like that. We always miss the fish fries, and I'm never there to make cakes and pies for the bake sales. But they'd do the same thing for us if *we* were the part of the Body that was suffering! Not because we were worthy or had earned special treatment or were indispensable—but just because we were a part of the Family of God!

As I started dinner, Bill sat down at the piano. [The children were quiet, knowing that a song was about to be born.] It wasn't long before the magnetism of the chorus Bill was singing drew me from the kitchen to the piano, and we finished the song that was to feed us better than any other food could have fed us:

> I'm so glad I'm a part of the Family of God!
> I've been washed in the fountain, cleansed by His blood.
> Joint heirs with Jesus as we travel this sod,
> For I'm part of the Family, the Family of God.
>
> You will notice we say brother and sister 'round here,
> It's because we're a Family and these folks are so near.
> When one has a heartache we all share the tears,
> And rejoice in each victory in this Family so dear.
>
> From the door of an orphanage to the house of the King,
> No longer an outcast, a new song I sing.
> From rags unto riches, from the weak to the strong,
> I'm not worthy to be here, but praise God I belong!

Since that Easter Sunday there have been heartaches and victories in our own lives that have been shared by the Family of God. It's been wonderful! . . . .

Ron is a very healthy, robust basketball coach these days. His life is a strong witness in our community to the power and love of Christ.

Reflection: Apart from our salvation, the most wonderful gifts God ever allowed us to receive are Christian brothers and sisters, who love us and who are loved by us in full measure as part of his family.

15

A Waitress
Inspires a Song

Song: *People Need the Lord*
Scripture: John 3:14–21
For God sent not his Son into the world to condemn the world; but that the world through him might be saved.

On New Providence Island, about 150 miles off the Florida coast, in a small Creole speaking church made up mostly of Haitians, two teenagers, Amy Terry and Tina Brown, stood to sing what often seems to missionaries to be the most meaningful song ever written. I had heard the song many times before, but my heart had never really "heard" it until that occasion, as I looked into the faces of those needy people.

The first time I was ever exposed to the song "People Need the Lord" was in Clearwater, Florida, many years before, when a young Oriental lad sang it in the Missions Conference at Trinity Baptist Church. It was not until August 1989 that I had any idea of its origin.

The two young men who wrote the song, Greg Nelson and Phil McHugh, are from the Midwest: Greg from Bismarck, North Dakota, and Phil from Aberdeen, South Dakota. Both are musicians who have been writing songs together for a number of years. They have written more than fifty as a team. Greg gave me the following account of the birth of their song:

> Phil and I were trying to write a song one day. We spent most of the morning talking about ideas. We decided, about lunch time, to go to a restaurant near my office in Nashville. After we were seated, a waitress came to our table. As she approached us and smiled, it seemed that her eyes were so empty. She was trying to convey a cheery attitude, but her face seemed to say something else. She took our order and walked away. Phil and I looked at each other and one of us said to the other, "She needs the Lord." We then began looking around the restaurant at all of the people there. They, too, seemed to have an emptiness in their faces. We sensed a real heaviness in our hearts as we watched them. Suddenly we realized that all of those people need the Lord. Just as quickly we both thought, *We need to write that—people need the Lord.*

We finished our meal and went back to my office and sat down to write what was in our hearts. The pictures from the restaurant that remained in our minds, coupled with the realization that millions of people around the world are also groping for some ray of light, gave rise to:

> Ev'ry day they pass me by, I can see it in their eye;
> Empty people filled with care, headed who knows where.
> On they go through private pain, living fear to fear.
> Laughter hides the silent cries only Jesus hears.

> We are called to take His light
>   to a world where wrong seems right;
> What could be too great a cost
>   for sharing life with one who's lost?
> Through His love our hearts can feel all the grief they bear.
> They must hear the words of life only we can share.

> *Chorus:*
> People need the Lord. People need the Lord.
> At the end of broken dreams, He's the open door.
> People need the Lord. People need the Lord.

When will we realize, people need the Lord?
(We need to give our lives, 'cause people need the Lord.)

Thus, this song was born and started its flight around the world. The element that makes it a favorite of almost everyone who hears it is the haunting melody that seems to drive its lyrics, the heart cry of lost humanity, right into our very souls.

Reflection: Every pastor, missionary, evangelist, and layman should be driven to others with the message of salvation through Christ—because all people really do need the Lord.

16

A Testimony
Circles the Globe

Song: *Heaven Came Down and Glory Filled My Soul*
Scripture: Matthew 16:21–28
*For the Son of man shall come in the glory of his Father
with his angels; and then he shall reward every man
according to his works.*

The Montrose Bible Conference Grounds in Montrose,
Pennsylvania, has been the sight of many wonderful Christian
experiences, but seemingly none quite so far-reaching as in the
summer of 1961. John W. Peterson says, "During one of the
sessions an opportunity for a time of personal testimonies was
given the audience, and Old Jim rose to his feet and told of his
conversion experience. In describing that night when he met
Christ, he used the phrase 'It seemed like Heaven came down
and glory filled my soul.' Right away I sensed that it would be
a fine title for a song, so I wrote it down and later in the week
completed the song. It became a favorite almost immediately."

Peterson feels that the title, the germ idea, is the most important part of a song. In order for a song to be effective and far-

reaching, the idea must be new, different, fresh, and with sparkle and appeal. It is not possible to predict that "something" that makes a song a winner. But the song born that day in 1961 has blessed the hearts of people all over America as well as on the mission fields worldwide.

John Peterson's songs come from a heart attuned to a goal of being a blessing to others through music. For Peterson, the message of a song is all-important. He says that his purpose, first and foremost, is to make Christ known.

Born in the little Swedish community of Lindsborg, Kansas, John was the youngest of seven children. He was eleven years of age when he received Christ as his personal Savior. From that time on, his grandfather, Charles Nelson, was a great spiritual influence in his life. At one point his grandfather said, "John, some day the Lord is going to use you with your writing." He was right on target with his prediction, because John W. Peterson has written more than one thousand songs and fifteen cantatas that have sold more than three million copies.

The world does not know the identity of "Old Jim," the white-haired gentleman who gave his testimony that day in Montrose, Pennsylvania, but there seems little doubt that he was used by God to prompt John Peterson to pen these words:

> O what a wonderful, wonderful day — Day I will never forget;
> After I'd wandered in darkness away, Jesus my Savior I met.
> O what a tender compassionate friend —
>   He met the need of my heart;
> Shadows dispelling, with joy I am telling,
> He made all the darkness depart!
>
> Now I've a hope that will surely endure —
>   After the passing of time;
> I have a future in Heaven for sure,
>   There in those mansions sublime.
> And it's because of that wonderful day —
>   When at the cross I believed;
> Riches eternal and blessings supernal,
> From His precious hand I received.

Chorus:
Heaven came down and glory filled my soul,
When at the cross the Savior made me whole;
My sins were washed away,
And my night was turned to day.
Heaven came down and glory filled my soul!

Why don't you, like young Peterson, set your sights and goals on being the best witness for the Savior you can possibly be, in whatever field of activity you follow?

Reflection: The glory that occasionally fills one's soul while on this earth is but a tiny foretaste of what awaits all those who have met Jesus Christ, have felt his compassionate love, and have been given the promise of "mansions sublime."

17

The *Deacon* Flies the Hump

Song: *It Took a Miracle*

Scripture: Psalm 36

Thy righteousness is like the great mountains; thy judgments are a great deep: O LORD, thou preservest man and beast.

Finding an Air Force pilot with the nickname of "Deacon" is quite unusual, but that was the case with John W. Peterson. This nickname was given to him because, every morning while in the military service, he sat on his footlocker and read his New Testament. Peterson was determined to live for the Lord, and did so unashamedly, whatever the circumstances.

These devotional periods stood Peterson in good stead when he flew the China Hump. He later said, "During those long, lonely flights I had wonderful opportunity for meditation and prayer. It always seemed that the Lord was very near. Perhaps there is no greater display of God's power and handiwork than the Himalaya Mountains. So often as I flew, while observing the rugged terrain below and the glories of the heavens above,

I was overwhelmed by the power of our Creator and the glory of his creation in general."

Obviously those flying days were later to inspire one of Peterson's greatest hymns of praise, as he explains in his own words:

Shortly after the war, while attending Bible School, I was in a missions class; and somehow, in a way that I can't quite remember, my thoughts were carried back to my "Hump-flying" days and the wonderful display of the power and handiwork of God there. Then the thought gripped me that the same God who created this universe with its never-ending wonders was the God who loved me and sent his only begotten Son to take my place on the cross. I was quite overwhelmed as I began to think of these two aspects of God's power and love; and suddenly, the words of a new song began to form in my heart. Before the class was over I had completely thought out the chorus and so I rushed out to one of the practice rooms in the music building; and there, within a very short time, I was sketching the words and melody of a new song.

> My Father is omnipotent,
> And that you can't deny;
> A God of might and miracles —
> 'Tis written in the sky.
>
> It took a miracle to put the stars in place,
> It took a miracle to hang the world in space;
> But when he saved my soul,
> Cleansed and made me whole,
> It took a miracle of love and grace!

Strangely enough, I was never quite satisfied with this number and I, probably more than anyone else, was surprised when it became such a favorite across the country and around the world. It, undoubtedly, was the song that the Lord used to establish me as a songwriter.

Unlike many young people today, young Peterson recognized God as the Almighty, Holy, Infinite One who is wonderful in his awesomeness. The trend of many today is to "human-ize" God and thus glorify man's accomplishments. But until we meet in eternity on a mystical common plane, God's glory is not fully comprehensible.

Never let it be said that you did not hold God in his rightful place. He loves you and wants to be your friend, but not your buddy or your pal. He must be recognized in your heart and life as the heavenly Father—omnipotent, omniscient, and omnipresent—"a God of might and miracles."

Reflection: Life takes on its fullest meaning only when we see God in all his beauty and holiness through the things that he has made.

18

The Blessings
of Humiliation

Song: *No One Understands Like Jesus*
Scripture: Hebrews 4:1–16
*For we have not an high priest which cannot be touched with
the feeling of our infirmities; but was in all points tempted
like as we are, yet without sin.*

John Peterson was not without his times of trial and
personal disappointment. He tells this story:

At one time I had a fairly responsible position with a certain
Christian organization. One day a supervisory position opened
up in my department. I was led to believe by one of my superi-
ors that I was to be promoted to this position. In my heart I felt
capable, with the help of the Lord, to handle a greater responsibility and I was thrilled at the challenge and prospect of the
new job. However, without advance notice, and to my utter
dismay and humiliation, I was passed by and a man from the
outside was brought in to fill the position.

There followed days of agonizing and heart-searching. I
could not help but feel like a complete failure. It was all that I

could do to keep from becoming bitter. The future looked dark and it seemed as if the Lord was putting me on the shelf, and by this was showing that he could not entrust any position of responsibility into my hands.

One night I had an occasion to spend an evening with the man who was brought in for my position. For some reason or other, though otherwise a very pleasant fellow, he became quite caustic in some of his remarks that night and I was deeply hurt. Later that evening, after returning home, I was sitting in our living room thinking about the events of the past days, thinking about the bitter experiences of that very evening, when I began to feel very alone and forsaken. Suddenly, I sensed the presence of the Lord in an unusual way and my mind was diverted from my difficulties to his faithfulness and sufficiency. Soon the thought occurred to me that he fully understood and sympathized with my situation; in fact, no one could ever completely understand or care as did he. Before long, an idea for the song came and I started to write:

No one understands like Jesus,
He's a friend beyond compare;
Meet him at the throne of mercy,
He is waiting for you there.
No one understands like Jesus,
When you falter on the way,
Tho' you fail Him, sadly fail Him,
He will pardon you today.

No one understands like Jesus,
When the days are dark and grim;
No one is so near, so dear as Jesus,
Cast your ev'ry care on Him.

You and I, along with John Peterson, can be thankful that the Bible says that Jesus Christ was tempted in all points as we are, yet was without sin. If I have a human need, Jesus has experienced it first. If I have a sorrow, Jesus has also experienced that. He shares in both my joys and my frustrations. Christ, as he lived here on the earth, was just as much man as if he had not been God, and just as much God as if he had not been man. That is why he is able to know the real me and have love, compassion, and even pity, for me — *and* for you.

Reflection: He is not truly exalted who is not exalted by Christ. The Lord sees you *now*, knows all about you *now*, and cares for you *now*. No one understands like Jesus!

19

They Wanted
to Change the Song

Song: *Over the Sunset Mountains*
Scripture: John 16:20–28
*And ye now therefore have sorrow: but I will see you again,
and your heart shall rejoice, and your joy no man taketh
from you.*

Out over Chicago, from radio station WMBI, located
at Moody Bible Institute, floated the beautiful strains of John
W. Peterson's song "Over the Sunset Mountains." It had been
written only a short time earlier. The audience reaction was
unusual, to say the least; requests began to pour in for copies of
the song. So encouraged was Peterson by the tremendous
response that he hired the services of an RCA recording studio
and proceeded to make a demonstration record, using the fine
talents of Bill Pierce and Dick Anthony. Here are those wonderful words:

> Over the sunset mountains,
> Someday I'll softly go;
> Into the arms of Jesus,
> He who has loved me so.

> Toiling will all be ended,
> Shadows will flee away;
> Sorrow will be forgotten—
> Oh, what a wonderful day!
>
> *Chorus*:
> Over the sunset mountains, Heaven awaits for me,
> Over the sunset mountains, Jesus, my Savior, I'll see.

In 1953 the song soon came to the attention of the executives of a famous sheet-music publisher. The company offered to publish the song, but expressed some reservations. They wanted the reference to Jesus eliminated so as to avoid offending certain religious groups. The idea of "Heaven" was fine, but not the reference to Jesus as Savior.

Though Peterson was young and inexperienced at the time, he had enough presence of mind to realize that this would weaken the message. Because he knew that the Bible teaches that Jesus Christ is the *only* way to heaven, he did not want to omit his name.

He left the publisher's office without signing a contract and was comforted in the belief that he had made the right decision. As he drove home, he began to write another song that later became his answer to the publisher. Its title was "My Song," and it began:

> I have no song to sing,
>   but that of Christ my King;
> to Him my praise I'll bring forevermore!
> His love beyond degree.
> His death that ransomed me;
>   now and eternally,
> I'll sing it o'er.

Both of these songs have blessed the hearts of thousands, in the United States and the world over.

The Christian world will be eternally grateful that John Peterson learned eternal values early in life, especially from his godly grandfather. While at Moody Bible Institute he learned the meaning of fellowshipping with the God who created the heavens and all the wonders on earth.

Reflection: One needs to be no more persuasive than when trying to convince himself. Blessed is the man who learns to drive a hard bargain with the "first person singular." Never let it be said that you sacrificed the joys and the benefits of the future on the altar of the immediate.

20

The Old Is Still New

Song: *Cornerstone*

Scripture: Ephesians 2:11–22

*Now therefore ye are no more strangers and foreigners, but
fellow citizens with the saints, and of the household of God;
And are built upon the foundation of the apostles and
prophets, Jesus Christ himself being the chief corner stone.*

Millions of people have been blessed by the music of
Lari Goss, even though at the time they were not aware of who
he was. Goss has orchestrated and conducted the accompani-
ment for more Christian recordings than almost any other person living today, but it was not until he had reached a pinnacle
of music acclaim among Christian musicians that the Lord
decided to send around the world a melody that he had given
to Lari.

Lari Goss was born to wonderful Christian parents in Car-
tersville, Georgia, in 1945. Although he started singing with his
family as a child, he was not given the opportunity of extensive
music training. Lari is self-taught, but what a musician! His
abilities are in demand by the leading music publishers of our
day.

He related the following story to me:

79

I had a melody that the Lord had given me that I called "Cornerstone." Yet I had no lyrics. At the same time I was studying the Word. [Lari is a marvelous student of the Bible.] I had been reading in Scriptures where Jesus is presented as the Chief Cornerstone. I reasoned with myself that maybe I could put that thought with my melody. The lyrics of the song came strictly from the inspiration of the Word of God. Most all of the phrases in the song are straight from Scripture.

I continued to work the melody and the Scriptures into each other. Then I went to the old hymnals to see what former writers had to say about Christ as a Stone or the Rock of our salvation. I borrowed a line from an old hymn—I don't even remember the song—"Where the seeds of truth are sown." Then I turned to that old favorite song, "Rock of Ages." It so ably depicted Christ as our Cornerstone, the Rock of Ages.

My mind then went to our security in the Lord. That led me to "Rock of Ages, so secure, for all time it shall endure. 'Til His children reach their home, He remains the Cornerstone."

No event or incident in my life influenced the song. It is strictly from the Scriptures:

> Jesus is the Cornerstone,
> Came for sinners to atone;
> Tho' rejected by His own
> He became the Cornerstone.

> When I am by sin oppressed,
> On the stone I am at rest;
> When the seeds of truth are sown
> He remains the Cornerstone.

> Rock of Ages, cleft for me,
> Let me hide myself in Thee.
> Rock of Ages, so secure,
> For all time it shall endure;
> 'Til His children reach their home,
> He remains the Cornerstone;
> 'Til the breaking of the dawn,
> 'Til all footsteps cease to roam.
> Ever let this truth be known,
> Jesus is the Cornerstone,
> Jesus is the Cornerstone.

Nancy Harmon, the noted traveling singer, was the first to record it, about two years after I had written it. It was nominated for a Dove Award in 1978 and still continues to be a favorite everywhere.

Reflection: No matter what your lot in life, if you are a Christian you are secure in the knowledge that the Lord Jesus Christ is the foundation and support of your very existence.

21

Driving Along,
Writing a Song

Song: *Where No One Stands Alone*
Scripture: Psalm 27
Hide not thy face far from me; put not thy servant away in anger: thou hast been my help; leave me not, neither forsake me, O God of my salvation.

In the year 1955, songwriter Mosie Lister was driving alone on a highway in northern Georgia, when all of a sudden he began singing:

> Hold my hand all the way,
> Every hour, every day,
> From here to the great unknown;
> Take my hand,
> Let me stand,
> Where no one stands alone.

Lister says, "I used to do a lot of my writing when I was driving by myself. Something about the rhythm of the car did something to my mind, so when I was alone I just started thinking about music and ideas. I have been writing songs since I was seventeen years old. I have written about five hundred songs."

Mosie Lister was born in Cochran, Georgia, in 1921. Lister, now associated with Lillenas Publishing Company in Kansas City, Missouri, has become quite famous as a songwriter and arranger. He is also director of publications for the Faith Music Catalog. For years he was an active choir director at the Riverside Baptist Church in Tampa, Florida, and still resides in that city.

Although Lister's two most popular songs are probably "How Long Has It Been?" and "'Til the Storm Passes By," the one selling the most records has been "Where No One Stands Alone." He explains how it came to be written:

> I started the chorus, "Hold my hand all the way . . ." and sang it all the way through. For about a year I only had the chorus, no verses. Finally, out of desperation, I wrote the verses. I tried to think of something that would lead up to "where no one stands alone" and then I remembered reading in the Psalms a theme that David wrote: "Hide not your face from me." That seemed to do something to my thinking. I sort of put myself in David's place. That is where the first verse came from. Once I had myself in the right frame of mind, the words came easily.

Thus was born Mosie Lister's beautiful song of consecration:

> Once I stood in the night with my head bowed low,
> In the darkness as black as could be;
> And my heart felt alone, and I cried,
> "Oh, Lord, don't hide your face from me."
>
> Like a king I may live in a palace so tall,
> With great riches to call my own;
> But I don't know a thing in this whole wide world
> That's worse than being alone.
>
> *Chorus*:
> Hold my hand all the way,
> Ev'ry hour, ev'ry day,

From here to the great unknown . . .
Take my hand,
Let me stand,
Where no one stands alone.

Did you ever think, Christian, that when you have Christ in your heart, you are never alone? We should always strive to maintain fellowship with him, drawing close to him every morning and every evening and never wandering farther than his fingertip all through the day. How exciting it is to realize that he actually lives within our hearts!

Reflection: God made you and me to fellowship with him and to love him—to hold his hand all the way. If, after receiving Christ as our personal Savior, we stray from him, we cease to fulfill the very reason for our existence.

22

Lost!
So Near to Safety

Song: *'Til the Storm Passes By*
Scripture: Psalm 107:13–34
*Then they cry unto the LORD in their trouble, and he
bringeth them out of their distresses.*

Mosie Lister says of his song "'Til the Storm Passes
By" that he wrote it "because a man in New York whom I had
known called me one day and asked me to write a song for
Mahalia Jackson." (Mrs. Jackson was especially popular for
her rendition of "He's Got the Whole World in His Hands.")

Lister grew up with people of minority groups, so when
Mahalia Jackson's name was mentioned, he remembered
something of her background and felt the right kind of song for
her fall perfectly into place in his mind. It contained the ideals
of struggling people. Lister explains, "I feel that this is something God gave me to say. Strangely enough, we could never
get her to sing it, but of course a lot of other people did. The
man who so very much wanted me to write it was never able to
do with it what he wanted to do, but still God used it."

The song has been a tremendous blessing to millions, including some Baptist missionaries who were camping a few years ago on a tiny island off the coast of New Guinea. They had gone there for an outing, a day of relaxation. The island was named Mbil Mbil and was only about three miles in circumference.

While going through the day's recreational activities, the supply of drinking water was exhausted. Suddenly the group realized that if they were to satisfy their thirst, they would have to go to the mainland and replenish their supply of water. Several volunteered to take the boat to the base island of New Guinea and bring back some water.

The stretch of sea between the volunteers and their destination was made without incident, but the return trip was quite a different story. They had no sooner filled their containers and boarded the boat when they noticed dark thunder clouds begin to roll in.

As they pushed the throttle to full-speed-ahead and made toward Mbil Mbil once again, the storm seemed to fall on them like a giant monster. The sky grew black and foreboding. The wind was so strong and the waves so tempestuous that the boat and all its passengers were immediately in jeopardy. Steering the boat was an impossibility. Soon it became evident that there was only one thing left to do and that was to turn the bow of the boat into the waves and try to keep the engine running.

The occupants of the boat began to pray fervently that God would spare their lives and guide them toward the tiny island, or at least toward land of some kind. All of a sudden, one of the fellows said, "Why don't we praise him?" Then, as the waves rolled and the wind howled about them, they began to sing Mosie Lister's song:

> In the dark of the midnight, have I oft hid my face,
> While the storms howl above me, and there's no hiding place.
> 'Mid the crash of the thunder, precious Lord, hear my cry;
> Keep me safe 'til the storm passes by.
>
> When the long night has ended, and the storms come no more,
> Let me stand in Thy presence on that bright, peaceful shore.

In that land where the tempest never comes, Lord, may I
Dwell with Thee when the storm passes by.

Chorus:
'Til the storm passes over, 'til the thunder sounds no more,
'Til the clouds roll forever from the sky.
Hold me fast; let me stand in the hollow of Thy hand.
Keep me safe 'til the storm passes by.

The report, later, was that God's presence filled the boat:
"We knew he was there. Our hearts were cheered. All of a sudden, one saw a flickering light on the island." It seems that
those who were left on the beach had guessed their problem
and had come out with a strong light. Eventually the storm-
tossed passengers made it to safety on the island.

Although there was a small prayer meeting on shore that
night, the next morning was a time when the whole group met
together for the worship service. They studied afresh and anew
and recognized in a more real sense how man is lost in the
storms of life and must always look to the heavenly Father for
guidance in every walk of life. Old truths took on new mean-
ings. They already knew what it meant to be lost in the darkness of sin and then saved by the Light of the World, but this
reality was accented by the experience of the night before.

Like those missionaries, if you know Jesus Christ as Savior,
then you must keep in mind that there are still others lost in the
sea of darkness and sin. They need your light on the beach of
safety.

Reflection: We cannot appreciate the security of knowing
Christ until we, through reading the Scriptures, become acutely
aware that many are in need of rescue and cannot find their
way to him. We can shine a welcoming beacon and guide them
to the Lord Jesus Christ.

23

From Ridicule
to a Reward

Song: *Each Step I Take*

Scripture: 1 Peter 2:20–25

*For even hereunto were ye called: because Christ also
suffered for us, leaving us an example, that ye should follow
his steps.*

"Mother, that is a beautiful song. Let's write to America and
get a copy." Those were the words of a young lad in the
Philippine Islands in 1962 as he listened with his mother to the
Lutheran Gospel Hour. His mother had recently become a
Christian and was being ridiculed for her newfound faith in
Christ by her husband and teenage son. On this particular
morning, a soloist on the radio program sang "Each Step I
Take," an unusual song written by Elmo Mercer.

The letter was soon on its way to the United States, and the
musical composition was returned to their home after a consid-
erable time. Having a copy of the song in hand made it even
more precious to the young man. In fact, he and his father
were both converted as a result of having the song sheet, and
the young lad later went on to study for the gospel ministry in
Manila.

"Each Step I Take" came during a dark period in the life of young Mercer and became one of his more famous songs. This was one of Mercer's first successful compositions, although he had been writing for five years at the time. His early efforts were the result of expressing exactly what he felt in his heart at the time. His mom and dad had brought him up in the church and he had learned the Scriptures very early.

Mercer has gone on to write more than one thousand songs, many of which have blessed the hearts of millions of people. His sincere desire is to be of service to Christ through the ministry of sacred songs, and his life is surrendered to Christ.

What about *your* life? Is it totally and completely surrendered to Christ? Is your life counting for him? Not everyone can write songs, but everyone can live a life of dedication to Christ. Everyone can live in a way that serves the Lord and brings honor and glory to God by following in Christ's footsteps and reflecting the words of Elmo Mercer's song:

> Each step I take my Savior goes before me,
> And with His loving hand He leads the way,
> And with each breath I whisper "I adore Thee,"
> Oh, what joy to walk with Him each day.
>
> I trust in God, no matter come what may,
> For life eternal is in His Hand,
> He holds the key that opens up the way,
> That will lead me to the promised land.

Reflection: God in his infinite wisdom does not allow us to see beyond today. In love he has thrown a veil across our way so that we cannot see what lies ahead. Therefore, we must walk with him each step of the way, trusting in him and leaning on him for every necessity of life. Can you say with Elmo Mercer, "Each step I take my Savior goes before me"?

24

Dayspring
in a Doctor's Office

Song: *The Way That He Loves*
Scripture: Romans 1:1–20
For the invisible things of him from the creation of the world are clearly seen, being understood by the things that are made, even his eternal power and Godhead; so that they are without excuse.

On Sunday morning, October 21, 1984, the audience of Lavon Drive Baptist Church sat eagerly anticipating the entrance of the "surprise singer." It was Surprise Sunday and a special preacher and singer had been invited, although their identities would not be known until they appeared on the platform.

At the specified time, in the early part of the service, Elmo Mercer approached the piano and began to play and sing his famous song "Each Step I Take." The audience was thrilled and responded with grateful appreciation that God had chosen to bless them through the songs of Elmo Mercer.

From Mercer's home in Nashville, Tennessee, or from his villa on Florida's east coast, comes a stream of original songs, choir arrangements, and musicals. This has continued for more than thirty-five years, much to the delight of millions of Americans.

Elmo and his wife, Marcia, also crisscross the country to direct music for revivals and conferences and to sing for church concerts. He writes for fourteen music companies, with nine different companies holding copyrights to his compositions. This talented servant of Christ retired in 1981 after spending more than thirty years as chief music editor for the Benson Company in Nashville. He also has had a number of piano and organ books published, and he and Marcia have recorded two cassette albums of songs.

One of Elmo's most tender, compassionate songs, "The Way That He Loves," was born when the Mercers had been married for three years and were expecting their first child. They were living in Winfield, Louisiana, at the time. Elmo had driven Marcia to the doctor's office for a routine check-up.

As young Mercer sat in the reception room waiting for his wife, he began thinking about the prospective blessings of the Lord on their young family. He also reflected on the bounty that God affords us in his magnificent world, all the reminders of his glorious love that he has made for us to enjoy.

A young budding songwriter is always alert to the inspiration of the hour as it suggests lyrics that sometimes come "like daysprings." Such an occasion was this, for—as Elmo sat waiting—God gave to him, in a few minutes, this wonderful song:

> The way that He loves is as fair as the day
> That blesses my way with light.
> The way that He loves is as soft as the breeze
> Caressing the trees at night.
> So tender and precious is He!
> Contented with Jesus I'll be.
> The way that He loves is so thrilling because
> His love reaches even me!
>
> The way that He loves is as deep as the sea,
> His Spirit shall be my stay.
> The way that He loves is as pure as a rose,

Much sweeter He grows each day.
His peace hovers near like a dove;
I know there's a heaven above.
To Jesus I'll cling, life's a wonderful thing
Because of the way He loves!

Reflection: How marvelous that, in addition to his perfect love, as expressed in our Savior, God has created for us a wonderful world in which to serve him through the talents he has given to us as individuals.

25

Joy for the Taking

Song: *Happiness Is the Lord*

Scripture: Psalm 144:9–15

Happy is that people, that is in such a case: yea, happy is that people, whose God is the LORD.

Ira F. Stanphill was born in Belview, New Mexico, in 1914. He has written more than 550 songs, the most popular of which are "Mansion over the Hilltop," "Room at the Cross," and, of course, "Happiness Is the Lord."

On any number of occasions the Lord has given a song to a songwriter when he or she least expected it. Such was the case with Ira Stanphill one afternoon in 1974 after he left the church office where he was pastor in Fort Worth, Texas.

The car radio was on, and as he rode along he listened to some commercial programs. Some were sponsored by establishments that advertised their "happy hour" and their alcoholic beverages. He also heard cigarettes being advertised in terms of how they bring happiness. The word *happiness* was used several times in the ads.

Ira related to me that he thought at the time that "happiness does not come with these things, but with knowing Christ." He continued, "As this thought really took over my mind I began to sing. I sang a new song, composing words and melody as I drove along. I sang it almost as it is published today."

Here, in Ira Stanphill's own words, is the rest of the story behind that song, "Happiness Is the Lord":

> As I reached home, I ran in with a broad smile. My wife asked, "What's the good news?" My answer was, "Well, I just got a song." "Let's hear it," she said. I told her that I didn't have it down yet, and so I went straight to the piano. In about fifteen to twenty minutes I had the finished work.
>
> I taught it to the people of my church. They picked it up quickly and sang it enthusiastically. So I mailed it to the Zondervan Corporation, the company for which I worked. They published it right away in several forms.
>
> It was introduced in Europe by a youth group from First Baptist Church of Dallas, Texas. It soon spread over Europe. Some years later, as I visited Nepal, I heard a group from England, also visiting in Nepal, sing my song:

> Happiness is to know the Savior,
> Living a life within His favor,
> Having a change in my behavior
> Happiness is the Lord.

> Happiness is a new creation,
> "Jesus and me" in close relation,
> Having a part in His salvation
> Happiness is the Lord.

> Real joy is mine, no matter if teardrops start;
> I've found the secret—it's Jesus in my heart!

> Happiness is to be forgiven,
> Living a life that's worth the livin',
> Taking a trip that leads to heaven
> Happiness is the Lord. Happiness is the Lord.
> Happiness is the LORD.

Reflection: If only everyone in the world could know the joy that comes through having a personal relationship with Christ.

26

From Suicide to Soulwinning

Song: *Room at the Cross for You*

Scripture: Proverbs 3:1–20

Trust in the LORD with all thine heart; and lean not unto thine own understanding. In all thy ways acknowledge him, and he shall direct thy paths.

A despairing young man, bent on taking his own life, found himself walking one day near a church where a service was being conducted by evangelist Willard Cantelon. Al Garr was directing the music for the service. The troubled young man had a gun in his pocket and was making his way toward a high bridge, not too far from the church. His intention was to shoot himself near the edge of the bridge, letting his body fall into the water.

As he passed the church, he heard Al Garr singing "There's Room at the Cross for You." He was so gripped by its message that he made his way into the church, postponing his mission of horror. There he found Christ as his Savior and was rescued from personal and spiritual disaster. "He later studied for the ministry and became an evangelist. A motion picture has been made of his life since that notable day when 'Room at the Cross for You' pointed him to Christ," says Ira Stanphill, pastor of the Rockwood Park Assembly of God in Fort Worth, Texas, and composer of that song and hundreds of others.

Because there is no such thing as luck or chance in the life of a Christian, I believe God drew this young man to himself, although he chose a very unusual method to do so.

The story of the song's birth is also unique. Ira Stanphill was preaching in a revival meeting in Kansas City, Missouri. As was his custom, he asked the people to submit suggested song titles while the congregation sang. As the choir presented their favorite selections, he would proceed to write a gospel song, using as the title one of those submitted by the audience.

On this particular Sunday morning, the people submitted about fifty ideas. Stanphill quickly thumbed through the titles and saw the words, "Room at the Cross for You." They struck a responsive chord and before the service was complete, he had given to the world a memorable song to fit that title.

Little did Stanphill realize at the time what an impact the song would have. In fact, he remembers that he thought the song would not go far. Probably because of that, he asked the people to come back that evening, promising that he would choose another one from the balance of titles and have another song ready. Although he spent much time choosing a title and was more cautious in forming the lyrics, the second song is not known at all. But "Room at the Cross for You" has been sung around the world.

Our lives are not lived by chance, but in either the permissive or directed will of God. Always watch for his direction in your life and accept those things that at the time seem unusual as a part of the handiwork of God. Learn to say with Fannie Crosby, "His purposes will ripen fast, unfolding every hour. The bud may have a bitter taste, but sweet will be the flower." We can be glad indeed that God directed Ira Stanphill to write these words of humble thanksgiving:

> The cross upon which Jesus died,
> Is a shelter in which we can hide,
> And its grace so free is sufficient for me

And deep is its fountain,
As wide as the sea.

Chorus:
There's room at the cross for you.
There's room at the cross for you;
Though millions have come,
There's still room for one.
Yes, there's room at the cross for you.

Reflection: Every day, before retiring, look back and recognize the hand of God as he quietly, tempestuously, strangely, or sometimes mysteriously moves to shape your life to make it more like his Son's. Trust him to lead you toward the paths of righteousness.

27

Much More to Come

Song: *Mansion over the Hilltop*
Scripture: Luke 12:27–34
Fear not, little flock; for it is your Father's good pleasure to give you the kingdom.

A young businessman stood one evening in 1945 in a revival meeting in Dallas, Texas, to give his testimony concerning God's blessings in his life. In the audience was a famous songwriter, Ira Stanphill; the evangelist was Gene Martin.

The businessman stated that his business had been in dire straits; it looked as if he would go completely under. Things were on the decline and had been for some time. Since the situation was completely beyond his ability to understand it or to do anything about, it had been thrusting him more and more into the depths of despair.

This man shared that he was a Christian and knew that the Lord had saved him, yet he did not understand why the Lord would allow these things to happen in his life. He was not accustomed to such financial reverses, but they could not be denied.

Then he told of how one day, for a period of diversion or

relaxation, he decided to get into his car and drive out into the country. He drove for miles, out beyond the busy streets and residential areas, into the country, where he stopped his car on a lonely road and continued on foot. Soon he found himself on a deserted, out-of-the-way trail and eventually came upon a dilapidated cottage. It was in great disrepair, with half the windows broken. Out front was a small girl, who played with a broken doll. Although the stuffing in the doll was protruding in several places, the child seemed to be content and happy.

He eased up to the front yard and called the little girl over and said to her, "Little girl, would you talk to me for a moment?" And she answered, "No!"

"Well," he said, "at least tell me how you can be happy living in such a house as that. It is broken down, the windows are out in many places, and that doll that you have in your hand—it is broken and the stuffing is coming out. How can you be happy?" The little girl looked up with her big, bright eyes and said, "Mister, you see, my daddy just came into a large sum of money and he is building us a brand new mansion over that hilltop."

The young businessman testified that those words pierced his heart. He realized for the first time that though his earthly business was shattered and in shambles, the heavenly Father had much greater things in store for him. It was as though he heard God himself saying, "Son, don't you know that I have a mansion prepared for you just beyond those clouds?" The young man concluded his story by telling how he went back home with a new determination to live for God, to let God take care of his business, and to look toward eternal things.

After hearing that young man speak, Ira Stanphill went home and slept that night, but rose early the next morning and went to the piano. With that story still fresh in his mind, he wrote the song "Mansion over the Hilltop." It has gone all across the country—in all our churches, in our homes—and has been recorded by scores of recording artists.

The Bible says that it has not even entered the heart of man, nor can we even conceive, all of the things that God has prepared for those that love him (1 Cor. 2:9). You may live in a humble home or even a small shack or cottage, but God has prepared greater and more beautiful things. We know that he has, because he says so in his Word. So don't be discouraged. Why don't you sing right now? Sing Ira Stanphill's words of joyful expectation:

> I'm satisfied with just a cottage below,
>   A little silver and a little gold;
> But in that city where the ransomed will shine,
>   I want a gold one that's silver lined.
>
> Tho' often tempted, tormented and tested,
>   And, like the prophet, my pillow a stone;
> And tho' I find here no permanent dwelling,
>   I know He'll give me a mansion my own.
>
> *Chorus*:
> I've got a mansion just over the hilltop.
>   In that bright land where we'll never grow old;
> And someday yonder we will nevermore wander,
>   But walk the streets that are purest gold.

Reflection: Nothing is judged superior except by comparison, and we will only be able to fully realize the excellence of all that God has prepared for us when we are able to compare it with all that we have on the earth now.

28

They Didn't Believe *Him,* Either

Song: *Follow Me*
Scripture: 1 Peter 5:1–11
Casting all your care upon him; for he careth for you.

A young newlywed once lay very ill and discouraged in a tiny shack on the back side of a mission compound in Africa. She and her young husband had left the United States to come to this place as medical missionaries.

Those first few weeks and months had been a tremendous struggle. Days that had turned to long agonizing weeks had been spent in building living quarters, pulling teeth, doctoring ulcers, and caring for multitudes of medical problems for these African nationals. Day after day they came for help with their problems and cares.

The husband ministered to their medical needs, but he also witnessed to their hearts and tried to bring them to Christ. He soon saw that he was able to help them medically, but he was not seeing souls come to know the Christ that had brought him to this place.

To add to the missionary's anxiety, his wife was sick and lay all day long in their little shack. The hardship and the struggle became too great and he began to give in to the pressures. His cry to God became, "Lord, get me out of this and I'll go back and be faithful. I'll pastor a small church and do your work. I just want to leave this place. I want my wife to be well. I still want to serve you, but not here. I am a failure in this mission field. I am not seeing people saved. I seem to be spending all my time pulling teeth and caring for the medical needs, so let me go back home, please."

But suddenly the picture changed, as the missionary explained later: "It seemed that I could almost see Christ; his message was so plain to me. I saw his wounded hands, and the blood still flowed from the wounds. His words to me were: 'I preached that same message in the streets of Jerusalem and in Palestine and they didn't believe me either. Why don't you just follow me and leave the results in my hands!'"

The once-despairing young man did just that. He received tremendous spiritual strength from the Lord's message to him and soon began to see people saved. His wife became well again. And out of the darkness came little sunbeams shining all around them. They became two of the greatest missionaries that their particular board had ever sent to the continent of Africa.

That story was given one night in a missionary conference in Grand Prairie, Texas, by Charles Greenaway. He, along with his wife, Mary, were the young couple that had gone to Africa many years before.

Ira Stanphill, the talented songwriter, was sitting in the audience. He went home and cried that night because he was so moved by the story. The next morning he went to his piano and, with tears streaming down his face, he penned:

> I traveled down a lonely road,
>   And no one seemed to care,
> The burden on my weary back,
>   Had bowed me to despair,
> I oft complained to Jesus,
>   How folks were treating me,

And then I heard Him say so tenderly,
"My feet were also weary,
   Upon the Calvary Road;
The cross became so heavy,
   I fell beneath the load,
Be faithful, weary pilgrim,
   The morning I can see,
Just lift your cross and follow close to Me."

"I work so hard for Jesus,"
   I often boast and say,
"I've sacrificed a lot of things,
   To walk the narrow way,
I gave up fame and fortune;
   I'm worth a lot to Thee,"
And then I heard Him gently say to me,
"I left the throne of glory,
   And counted it but loss,
My hands were nailed in anger,
   Upon a cruel cross,
But now we'll make the journey,
   With your hand safe in Mine,
So lift your cross and follow close to Me."

God does not always provide an easy life for us, but his message is just the same as it was to the apostle Paul: "My grace is sufficient for thee." Though we, like Paul, may implore the Lord to deliver us from trials and tribulations that beset us, he may be using these things to cause us to be hardened, strong, and useful servants in his loving hands. We need only heed that awesome challenge: "Follow me."

Reflection: Never forget that God sees you and knows all about you. And he *cares* for you. Your extremity is his opportunity to forge you into the person he wants you to be.

29

God Led Her
to the Poor Farm

Song: *God Leads His Dear Children Along*
Scripture: Psalm 16
*Thou wilt shew me the path of life: in thy presence is fulness
of joy; at thy right hand there are pleasures for evermore.*

Haldor Lillenas, founder of a noted music-publishing
company, made his way to the United States from Scandinavia
more than fifty years ago. His first years in this country were
hard, but a kind lady befriended him and taught him the
English language. More importantly, perhaps, she told him the
story of Christ and led him to know the Savior in his heart.
Many times, she sang to him a comforting song entitled "God
Leads His Dear Children Along."

Lillenas's travels eventually landed him in Kansas City,
Missouri, where he started his music company. Years later, he
began thinking about the song that had been so meaningful to
him in his youth and decided to find out something about its
writer, C. A. Young. After many letters and phone calls, he discovered that the songwriter had passed away, but that his
widow was living in a nearby town. He wondered if she could

shed some light on the story behind the song that still touched his heart so often.

Shortly thereafter, Haldor drove out to the little town, with only her name and an address someone had located for him. He stopped first at a service station, where a young man came running up to the car and asked with a smile, "May I help you?" Lillenas asked for directions to the address he held in his hand. The young man's countenance fell as he replied, "Sir, that's the county poor farm."

Lillenas's first reaction was to have the lad fill up the gas tank and then to make his way back to his office. He remembered thinking, "I just cannot go talk to a lady about God's leadership, when she has been led to the poor farm." But, after getting the gasoline, he changed his mind and decided, "I'll at least go by and see her for a few moments, as long as I'm here."

Haldor followed the young man's directions to the poor farm, approaching the buildings with some hesitation and doubt. He was led to Mrs. Young's room and explained who he was and why he had come. Her immediate response was, "Oh, Mr. Lillenas, it's so wonderful of you to come out and visit me!" Her radiant enthusiasm suddenly changed his whole attitude toward the visit, and his excitement mounted as she told him this story:

> My husband and I were married while we were very young. God gave us a wonderful life together; he led us from day to day. We had so much of Jesus. But then God took my husband. Now God has led me here, and I'm so excited and glad about it! God has used me in this place. Isn't it wonderful that God leads his children day by day and step by step? Many people come to this place and they are so sad and in such great need. They need help and comfort. I have been able to cheer many of them and lead scores of them to the Lord Jesus Christ. How thankful I am that God has brought me to this place, where I can be of so much help to these people!

Haldor Lillenas was deeply moved by Mrs. Young's words and excited that he had found more than just a story behind a gospel song. He had found a Christian woman completely surrendered to God's will for her life. For a few brief moments, he had shared the joy she felt in such sweet surrender. The third verse of her husband's beloved song meant even more to him after that day:

> Away from the mire, away from the clay,
> God leads His dear children along.
> Away up in Glory, eternity's day;
> God leads His dear children along.
>
> *Chorus*:
> Some through the waters, some through the flood,
> Some through the fire, but all through the blood;
> Some through great sorrow, but God gives a song,
> In the night's season and all the day long.

Reflection: A Christian is never more peaceful and happy than when experiencing the day-by-day leadership and loving care of the Good Shepherd and sharing that godly heritage by serving others in his name.

30

God Reveals Himself

Song: *How Great Thou Art*

Scripture: Psalm 8

O LORD our LORD, how excellent is thy name in all the earth! who hast set thy glory above the heavens.

"How Great Thou Art" is probably the all-time favorite hymn today. Although its origin had roots in Europe, it was not widely known until 1957, when the Billy Graham Crusade in New York City launched it on a never-ending spiral around the world. It was performed nearly a hundred times during those meetings and countless times ever since. Many marvelous things could be said of the accomplishments of this song, which has brought thousands to Christ. This great hymn has a history that stretches back over a hundred years.

The original song was written by a young Swedish preacher, Carl Boberg, and first published in 1886, under the title *"O Store Gud."* Boberg wrote a poem, not meaning to write a hymn, but later heard it being sung to an old Swedish tune.

More than forty years later, an English missionary first heard the song in Russia. Stuart Hine, born in 1899, in Hammersmith Grove, a small hamlet in England, was dedicated to the Lord by his parents in a Salvation Army meeting. He was led to Christ by Madame Annie Ryall, on February 22, 1914, and was baptized shortly thereafter. In his teen years, Hine was introduced more fully to music as a member of the Towner Hamlet Choir. He was also influenced greatly by the teaching of Charles H. Spurgeon. At age eighteen he joined the English armed forces and served for a time in France.

Hine was married on June 20, 1923. Nine years later, he and his young wife went as missionaries to the Carpathian area of Russia, then a part of Czechoslovakia. There, they heard a very meaningful hymn that happened to be a Russian translation of Carl Boberg's *"O Store Gud"* (O Great God). The translation was by I. S. Prokhanow, a giant in the evangelical movement in Russia just past the turn of the century.

While ministering in the Carpathian Mountains, Hine found himself in the midst of a threatening storm. The thunder, as it rolled through the mountain range, was so awesome that it reminded Hine of the beautiful Russian hymn that had already become so dear to him. English verses began to form in his mind, verses that were suggested by portions of the Russian translation. Some time later, a second verse was written as Hine wandered through the forests and woodlands of Romania with some of the young people of that region. A third verse was written before returning to England.

In 1948, Stuart Hine and David Griffiths visited a camp in Sussex, England, where displaced Russians were being held. Only two in the whole camp knew Christ as Savior and would profess their belief. The testimony of one of the two, and his anticipation of the second coming of Christ, inspired Hine to write the fourth stanza of his English version of the hymn.

In his book, *Not You, But God*, published in 1982, Hine presents two additional, optional verses that he copyrighted in 1958. The other portion of the hymn was copyrighted in 1953, as a translation of the Russian version.

Dr. J. Edwin Orr introduced Hine's "How Great Thou Art" in the United States in 1954. Three years later, it began its orbit around the world by way of the New York Crusade and has touched millions since then.

In a letter from his daughter, Sonia Hine, dated March 16, 1989, was the somber news that Stuart Hine had died peacefully in his sleep two days before. He was ninety-two years of age. His memorial service was held at the Gospel Hall on Martello Road, Walton-on-Naze, Essex, England, on March 23, at two o'clock in the afternoon.

Thus, in quiet dignity, ended the life on earth of a man whose long years had been dedicated to serving the Lord. He left to peoples around the world no more fitting heritage than the words he wrote to this glorious hymn of praise:

O Lord my God! When I in awesome wonder,
Consider all the works [worlds] Thy hand hath made,
I see the stars, I hear the rolling thunder,
Thy pow'r throughout the universe displayed.

Chorus:
Then sings my soul, my Savior God to Thee;
How great Thou art! How great Thou art!
Then sings my soul, my Savior God to Thee;
How great Thou art! How great Thou art!

Reflection: Each time you hear a bird sing, hear the thunder roll, or see a babbling brook, be reminded, like Stuart Hine, of God's greatness and the love he extends so mercifully to his people.

31

It Started by the Creek Bank

Song: *We Shall Behold Him*

Scripture: Revelation 1:1–7

Behold, he cometh with clouds; and every eye shall see him, and they also which pierced him: and all kindreds of the earth shall wail because of him. Even so, Amen.

The small rural town of Madisonville, Kentucky, gave to the world one of the all-time great gospel songwriters, Dottie Rambo. Songs that are so meaningful to Christians everywhere seem literally to flow from her pen. There seems to be no end to the list of favorites.

It all started when Dottie was only eight years of age. She came home one day and began to quote a poem to her mother, who was cooking in the kitchen. She had just written it down by the creek bank. Her mother began to weep with joy as she realized that her little girl, one of her eleven children, had a wonderful gift from the Lord. At age eleven she wrote a song that was sung by the Happy Goodman Family and recorded by Governor Jimmy Davis of Louisiana.

For the next thirty-six years, God gave Dottie Rambo hundreds of marvelous songs, still being sung by people around the world. Along the way there were many heartaches and disappointments scattered among those triumphs. Yet, out of those periods of hurting, God gave some of her most blessed songs!

In 1981, Dottie reached what seems to be the zenith of her writing career. She was singing with her husband, Buck, and another young lady in a tent revival in Ohio. She and the young lady were traveling to the large tent from their motel room. Buck had gone on ahead with the ministers. Let's have her tell the story:

> As we pulled out of the driveway of the motel it was about time for the sun to set. I looked up and saw one of the most beautiful and unusual cloud formations. I have always loved beautiful cloud formations and have often been fascinated when I saw a formation that resembled a person or an object. I sensed as I watched that the Lord was about to give me something wonderful for the church. I saw colors that I had never seen in my lifetime. It seemed that the clouds almost took on the form of angels. The colors were so brilliant and unusual— blues, azures, and amber.
>
> Presently the clouds parted and there seemed to be a straight passageway through the formation. By this time I was weeping so much that I couldn't see to drive. It seemed, as the clouds parted, as if I could see the Savior coming in the clouds, with trumpets sounding.
>
> I said to my young companion, "Patty, you're going to have to drive. I can no longer see." We changed places and we continued to drive. Patty asked, "What is wrong? Are you sick?" She didn't know that the Lord was giving me a song. It was being written in my heart because I had nothing on which to write.
>
> I then said, "Patty, would you like to hear what the Lord just gave to me?" I began to sing my song. Soon she was weeping and had to pull the car to the side of the road. We were a little late to church that night, but before we reached the tent the Lord had given me the whole song. When I got there I could play the entire piece on my guitar. Every phrase was exactly as it should be. Changes were not necessary. It just came like a dayspring:

The sky shall unfold, preparing His entrance;
The stars will applaud Him with thunders of praise;
The sweet light in His eyes shall enhance those awaiting;
And we shall behold Him then, face to face.

The angel shall sound the shout of His coming;
The sleeping will rise from their slumbering place;
And those who remain shall be changed in a moment;
And we shall behold Him then, face to face.

Chorus:
We shall behold Him, we shall behold Him,
Face to face, in all of His glory.
We shall behold Him, we shall behold Him,
Face to face, our Savior and Lord.

Sandi Patti recorded "We Shall Behold Him" and helped make the song known in almost every nook and cranny of our nation. Because of this song, Sandi Patti was named Vocalist of the Year in 1981. In that same year, Dottie Rambo received Dove awards as Songwriter of the Year and the song itself was named Song of the Year.

Thank you, Dottie Rambo, for giving to the world this marvelous Christian song.

Reflection: The Lord's coming is the beginning of an eternity of joy for every Christian. What a marvelous day when we behold the Savior—"Face to face, in all His glory"!

32

One Sadness,
Two Songs

Songs: *He Looked Beyond My Fault*
       If That Isn't Love

Scripture: Isaiah 53:1–12

*But he was wounded for our transgressions, he was bruised
for our iniquities: the chastisement of our peace was upon
him; and with his stripes we are healed.*

A crushing sorrow in the life of Dottie Rambo gave
birth to two of her most famous songs. Here is her own story
as she related it:

> My brother was a sinner boy. He had never been a
> Christian, but he and I were very close. We double-dated when
> we were young, although he was two years older. He always
> would come to hear me sing, but would leave before the invita-
> tion of the service.
> During the time I was writing both of these songs, Eddy was
> dying with cancer. He had become a very wicked boy, but I
> loved him very much. So, I went to the hospital to see him.
> They had brought him to Nashville to die.
> I went into the room. They had him in a ward with another
> man. I pulled the curtain around his bed and sat down and

started talking to him. I said, "Darling, the doctors say unless a miracle happens or unless this drug works, you have only about five or six weeks to live." None of my family would tell him. I knew he was lost, and I decided along with my mother that I must level with him. He began to cry and said, "But Sis, I've been so wicked. I've been in prison. I've been a gambler and a thief and everything that goes along with that. I am just too wicked for God to save me." I started witnessing to Eddy and praying with him. But he could find no peace.

A few days later, as I sat alone in a rocking chair in my living room at home, praying for Eddy, the Lord impressed on me that he wanted to give me some words to give to Eddy. The lyrics began to come.

I went back to Eddy and said, "Darling, I have some words for you." [By then she had the melody, an old English tune.] I stood over his bed. By this time he weighed only sixty-five pounds. I started to sing:

> Amazing Grace shall always be my song of praise;
> For it was grace that bought my liberty.
> I do not know just why he came to love me so;
> He looked beyond my fault and saw my need.
>
> I shall forever lift mine eyes to Calvary,
> To view the cross where Jesus died for me.
> How marvelous the grace that caught my falling soul.
> He looked beyond my fault and saw my need.

He started weeping and wanted me to write the words down. I did so and left them with him.

A few days later, I went to Cleveland, Tennessee, to sing in a Baptist church. I asked for prayer for Eddy. As the minister began to speak, following the music, at about eleven o'clock, I sat down. I thought of Eddy, but the tears were not there. All of a sudden, I sensed that Eddy was fine. A beautiful peace came over me. The Lord just seemed to let me know that Eddy was okay.

The next day I returned and went to see Eddy, but now they had taken him home to spend his final days. I walked into his room and said, "I have some good news. I want to tell you something." He said, "Sis, before you do, I want to tell *you* something. Yesterday at about eleven o'clock, I really found my peace with God."

The Lord had really saved him. The song became alive to me. I realized what God had done. I began to tell Eddy about love and what the love of God had done. God's love is so far beyond us. I told him about the thief on the cross beside Jesus, who was saved and had no chance to have a personal testimony or to even be baptized. Yet Jesus said to him, "This day thou shalt be with me in Paradise."

Through all of this the Lord directed me to write:

He left the splendor of Heaven, knowing His destiny
Was the lonely hill of Golgotha—there to lay down His life for
  me.

Chorus:
If that isn't love, the ocean is dry,
There are no stars in the sky, and the sparrow can't fly!
If that isn't love, then Heaven's a myth,
There's no feeling like this, if that isn't love!

Reflection: In spite of all we do, no matter how hard we try, we can never understand why the Lord would love us so—why he would express it and show it to us in so many ways.

33

Thirteen Cents
on the Contract

Song: *Remind Me, Dear Lord*
Scripture: Psalm 143
I remember the days of old; I meditate on all thy works; I muse on the work of thy hands.

Early in the ministry of Buck and Dottie Rambo, God unmistakably showed her his direction in their lives. When the way ahead was foggy, God chose what would be to some an insignificant act to guide their decision making. Consider Dottie's story about her song "Remind Me, Dear Lord":

> At the time I wrote this song, we were living in Kentucky just getting started in the music ministry. Both my husband and I were holding down jobs and singing on the weekends. We received a call from John T. Benson. We called him "Pop." He called about having me sign a writer's contract to have our family sing for him.
>
> We didn't know about contracts or what to do about such things. Since it was only a hundred miles from Nashville, my

husband, Buck, and my daughter, Reba, and I drove to see Pop
Benson. As we traveled I prayed: "Lord, we don't know anything about contracts, so you will have to lead us. If we are to
sign the contract, let it read so many hundred dollars and thirteen cents. If you'll just let thirteen cents be the last numbers on
the contract, then I'll know that we are supposed to sign it." I
told no one about my prayer, not even Buck.

When we arrived we began looking over the contract. We
were looking at all the details. Buck was reading it, but I was
trying to find out the amount. I said, "Let me look at it." Mr.
Benson looked over his glasses and said, "Well, Dot, my girl,
this is the best I can do." I really wasn't interested in anything
except that *"thirteen cents."* When I looked at the amount it read
so many dollars and "thirteen cents"! When I saw that I said,
"Give me a pencil." Buck said, "Wait a minute, we haven't read
it that well. We don't know that much about it." I said, "We
don't need to know anything else. We are just supposed to sign
it." So we signed it.

We got into our car and began pulling away from the curb.
All of a sudden, I began talking quietly to the Lord. I said:
"Lord, I appreciate your doing this for me. I know you must
have done a million things like this that I didn't know about or
didn't remember and haven't thanked you for, but you know
me and I'm human and I forget. But when you do good things,
just roll back the curtain and remind me of them and I'll thank
you for them!"

When that happened the melody in my heart started rolling
and I started weeping. Buck put on the brakes and said, "What
is wrong with you?" I said, "Nothing, I'm just rejoicing. I'm
writing a song." During the one hundred miles home, without
an instrument, I wrote:

> The things that I love and hold dear to my heart
> Are just borrowed—they're not mine at all.
> Jesus only let me use them to brighten my life.
> So remind me, remind me, dear Lord.
>
> Roll back the curtain of mem'ry now and then;
> Show me where You brought me from and where I could
>   have been.

Remember I'm human, and humans forget;
So remind me, remind me, dear Lord.

Reflection: One of our deplorable weaknesses as human beings is that we are so forgetful of his blessings and his watch-care. May we do all in our power to cease this terrible habit by opening our hearts to his loving reminders.

34

From the Storm Comes a Song

Song: *Sheltered in the Arms of God*

Scripture: Psalm 61

For thou hast been a shelter for me, and a strong tower from the enemy. I will abide in thy tabernacle for ever: I will trust in the covert of thy wings. Selah.

The winds were howling and Dottie Rambo walked along the beach among the scattered pieces of driftwood. A small fire flickered nearby, and not far away were the watchful eyes of her loving husband, Buck. This was another of those times when Dottie wanted to be alone to ponder the thoughts that troubled her very soul. An unfaithful friend had caused a very sad disappointment. But out of such troubled times, a song usually appeared. One was ever so near at that moment, in the heart of this woman who had been writing songs since she was nine years old. Dottie tells us about the song born that day:

> There had been a real bad storm. The driftwood had been piled everywhere on the beach, and I was going through a time that was a low valley for me. It was sort of a storm in my own

119

life. The white caps were really breaking across the water. As I walked among the driftwood and the seaweed, my guitar was strapped over my shoulder and I was contemplating the lyrics of several songs that the Lord seemed to be giving me at the time. All of a sudden, I felt, "Lord, this storm is so much like my life, and yet, in the midst of the storms of life, Lord, you have been a shelter to me, and when I can't take the storm, I run to you for that shelter and, suddenly, I feel secure."

While thinking on those things, and watching the storm as it kicked up the waters, I began to write a song. The melody was coming as I played my guitar, but I could not find an opening for the song, I could not find a way to interpret the song, something that would give it a springboard.

As I continued to walk, I pled with the Lord, "Lord, how am I going to start this song?" And, as I was talking to God, the closeness of the Lord touched me on the shoulder. I felt his presence, so real. I had a very warm feeling and these words came forth: "Thank you, Lord, I feel the touch of your hand, so kind and tender." Then I started to weep and said, "Lord, that is how I will open the song."

As she continued to walk, the words kept coming and finally God had given Dottie Rambo a message for her own troubled heart. This message can also be for you. Why don't you sing it right now, if you know the familiar melody. If not, speak the words softly, as a prayer:

> I feel the touch of hands, so kind and tender,
> They're leading me in paths that I must trod;
> I have no fear when Jesus walks beside me,
> For I'm sheltered in the arms of God.

> Soon I shall hear the call from Heaven's portals,
> "Come home, my child, it's the last mile you must trod."
> I'll fall asleep and wake in God's new Heaven,
> Sheltered safe within the arms of God.

> *Chorus*:
> So let the storms rage high, the dark clouds rise;
> They won't worry me.

For I'm sheltered safe within the arms of God;
He walks with me, and naught of earth shall harm me,
For I'm sheltered in the arms of God.

Perhaps there is a storm in your life. Maybe it brings heartache or fear. As you draw ever so close to the Lord Jesus through the reading of his Word, you, too, will find the touch of his hand, "so kind and tender."

Reflection: There are days so dark that we seek in vain for the face of our Friend Divine. But though darkness covers our world, he is there to guide, by the touch of his hand and the light of his Word.

35

Singing About the Cross

Song: *I Will Glory in the Cross*
Scripture: Galatians 6:1–15
But God forbid that I should glory, save in the cross of our Lord Jesus Christ, by whom the world is crucified unto me, and I unto the world.

Dottie Rambo once said, "I asked the Lord to let me, at least once each year, write a song that will speak to the hearts of Christians everywhere." Her songs might not have come with that exact frequency, but in the Lord's time he gave to all of us, through her, so many wonderful compositions. She recently told me the following story:

> Buck and I were going through the only rough time in our marriage. We were doing a lot of concerts, competitive concerts, making a lot of money. Suddenly I realized that I was not living close to the Lord. I was not writing under the anointing of the Holy Spirit. I also realized that I had never done anything to merit all of this goodness, recognition, and fame.
>
> I then began to study the Scriptures where Paul said that he

didn't glory in himself [Gal. 6:14]. I came back to the realization that all I have is because of the grace of God and the cross of Christ.

During this time we went to Holland to do a number of concerts. When we got off the plane, people met us and took us to this little quaint hotel. As we rode along they informed us that while we were there, singing in the concerts, we were not to sing about the cross of Christ. I looked at the young man who was escorting us and asked, "Do you mean we are not allowed to sing about the cross to these Christians?" He said, "No, they consider it gory. They don't want to hear about the blood or the cross." I looked at this young man—I was old enough to be his mother—and said, "Son, if you won't tell them you told me this, then I will pretend I don't know it. Because I *will* be singing about the cross and about the blood of Christ."

We sang in the concert that very night, "He Looked Beyond My Fault and Saw My Need." People were weeping all over the audience, even the man who said that we couldn't sing about the cross of Christ. The Lord really seemed to move in the hearts of the people.

We went back to the little hotel that night and to bed. I lay there in the dark. Buck, I thought, was asleep. I began to weep and I said, "God, I apologize that we are so stupid that we wouldn't want to hear about the blood of Christ, his cross, and his grace. I really apologize." As I lay there in the darkness the Lord gave me:

> I boast not of works, nor tell of good deeds.
> For naught have I done to merit His grace.
> All glory and praise shall rest upon Him,
> So willing to die in my place.

> My trophies and crowns, my robe stained with sin;
> T'was all that I had to lay at His feet.
> Unworthy to eat from the table of life,
> 'Til love made provision for me!

> I will glory in the cross, in the cross,
> Lest His suff'ring all be in vain.
> I will weep no more for the cross that He bore.
> I will glory in the cross.

I had to keep it in my heart and in my mind until the next morning, when I awoke to write it down.

What an amazing story and what a glorious song!

Reflection: I, too, have nothing in which to glory, save in the blessed truth of the death, burial, and resurrection of our blessed Lord. By his marvelous grace he included me—and you—in his kingdom.

36

Echoes
from the Past

Song: *Make Me a Blessing*

Scripture: 2 Corinthians 1:1–7

Who comforteth us in all our tribulation, that we may be able to comfort them which are in any trouble, by the comfort wherewith we ourselves are comforted of God.

Ira B. Wilson once startled his friends by saying, "I don't remember writing the lyrics to that song." He said that until his death, yet his song lives on in the hearts of Christians everywhere.

George Shuler and Ira Wilson were roommates at Moody Bible Institute in 1924. There they combined their talents and gave the world a beautiful song of consecration, "Make Me a Blessing." Wilson wrote the lyrics and Shuler the musical setting.

At first the song was rejected by musical publishers, so Shuler had one thousand copies printed to distribute on his own. One fell into the hands of George Dibble, an outstanding singer who was at that time music director for the International Sunday School Convention in Cleveland, Ohio. Dibble asked for permission to use the song and it was granted. Soon people everywhere were singing it, and publishers were wanting to distribute copies. Its popularity has grown since then until Christians everywhere can sing "Make Me a Blessing," perhaps even by memory.

Between the time Ira Wilson wrote the lyrics and the time the song began to be so well known, Wilson apparently forgot that he was the author. Until he died, he never remembered that he had written these famous words:

> Out in the highways and byways of life,
> Many are weary and sad;
> Carry the sunshine where darkness is rife,
> Making the sorrowing glad.
>
> Give as 'twas given to you in your need,
> Love as the Master loved you;
> Be to the helpless a helper indeed,
> Unto your mission be true.

This song should be the heart cry of Christians everywhere. It should be our desire to be a blessing to others. We can do that in many, many ways. We can tell others about the Savior. We can also help others by providing for the poor. Never has the world needed you more than during this time, so why don't you adopt "Make Me a Blessing" as your prayer and your reason for living?

Reflection: "Others, Lord, yes others. Let this my motto be. Help me to live for others, that I may live like Thee." We cannot truly serve Christ apart from helping others and reflecting his light wherever we go.

37

The Fruits
of Persistence

Song: *Overshadowed*
Scripture: Psalm 46
God is our refuge and strength, a very present help in trouble.

George Shuler, formerly a music-faculty member of the Moody Bible Institute, was playing the organ one day during a service at the famous Moody Church in Chicago. Sometime during the service the speaker prayed aloud, "O Lord, over-shadow us." This thought stuck with young Shuler, and after the service he went to his studio and wrote the words and music of what is now the refrain of the popular gospel song "Overshadowed." He knew that he needed some verses to accompany the chorus, so he contacted Dr. H. A. Ironside, the pastor, asking him if he might write them. Dr. Ironside post-poned the project for about two years.

Finally, Shuler, in desperation, asked Dr. Ironside's secretary to prompt him to write the verses. Her constant reminders caused him to finally write the poem and then say, "Now, stop pestering me!" Shuler took the words and proceeded to publish them as a song that winged its way around the world and has been a wonderful blessing to many Christians. It is a favorite song of many thousands.

George Shuler was born in New York City approximately a century ago. He has written many songs, not the least of which is "Overshadowed":

> How desolate my life would be,
> How dark and drear my nights and days,
> If Jesus' face I did not see
> To brighten all earth's weary ways.
>
> Now judgment fears no more alarm,
> I dread not death, nor Satan's pow'r;
> The world for me has lost its charm,
> God's grace sustains me ev'ry hour.
>
> *Chorus*:
> I'm overshadowed by His mighty love,
> Love eternal, changeless, pure.
> Overshadowed by His mighty love,
> Love is mine, serene, secure.
> He died to ransom me from sin
> He lives to keep me day by day.
> I'm overshadowed by His mighty love,
> Love that brightens all my ways.

Never hesitate to do today what your heart finds to do for the Lord Jesus Christ. Don't keep putting off things that need to be done for the Savior, for your efforts may live for eternity.

Reflection: How comforting it is to know that God, the Creator who pushed up the mountains and scooped out the valleys and filled the oceans of the world, sees and knows about you and me every hour. Truly he overshadows us with his mighty protecting arms and covers us with his everlasting love and grace.

38

God's Greatest Gift

Song: *Hark! the Herald Angels Sing*
Scripture: Luke 2:13–18
Glory to God in the highest, and on earth peace, good will toward men.

Like a distant purple mountain protruding through a pillow of white cloud, Charles Wesley stands head and shoulders above that grand group we call "gospel songwriters." He knew that music is one of our most wonderful methods of praising God and that singing in adoration and worship is mentioned repeatedly in the Scriptures. Every person should develop a loving appreciation for the songs that honor Christ and worship the Father.

Charles Wesley, like many other famous songwriters, began his ventures into verse-making at an early age. Born in England in 1707, he followed his father and older brother, John, in studying for the ministry. In the 1730s, shortly after Charles's ordination, the two brothers made a journey to America with Governor Oglethorpe. Charles Wesley was, at that time, the governor's secretary. On the way over, the brothers were influenced greatly by the Christian piety of a group of

Moravians. This probably led to the evangelical conversion of both the Wesleys. A year later they returned to their own country, where they banded together as itinerant preachers to spread a message of deliverance to a wicked and rebellious people, thus establishing the roots of the Methodist Revival.

John, the leader of the two and usually the spokesman, had seven rules for singing:

1. Learn the tune.
2. Sing the words as they are printed.
3. Sing all. If it is a cross, take it up and you will find a blessing.
4. Sing lustily and with good courage.
5. Sing modestly. Do not bawl.
6. Sing in time. Do not run before or stay behind.
7. Above all, sing spiritually. Have an eye to God in every word.

Charles wrote his first hymn just three days after his conversion. That hymn was "O for a Thousand Tongues to Sing." What a testimony to his salvation! As the years passed, he is said to have written 6,500 hymns and gospel songs on every conceivable subject. One of the most famous of his hymns is the Christmas carol "Hark! the Herald Angels Sing," written in 1738, about one year after his conversion. It is almost impossible to pick up a church hymnal today and find it omitted. Many other wonderful songs flowed from his fluent pen: "Jesus, Lover of My Soul," "Christ, the Lord, Is Risen Today," and "Love Divine, All Loves Excelling," to name a few.

It is said that no other man swayed the minds of the people of England as did John Wesley. Yet, the sermons of John are silenced and forgotten in England today, while the songs of his brother Charles are heard and sung around the world. Probably none is so familiar as:

> Hark! the herald angels sing,
> "Glory to the new-born King;
> Peace on earth, and mercy mild;

God and sinners reconciled!"
Joyful, all ye nations, rise,
Join the triumph of the skies;
With angelic hosts proclaim,
"Christ is born in Bethlehem!"
Hark! the herald angels sing,
"Glory to the new-born King."

Reflection: Sending his Son is God's way of bringing fallen men back to himself—"God and sinners reconciled." Is that what Christmas means to you?

39

Goldie Encouraged Him

Song: *I'll Fly Away*
Scripture: Psalm 55:1–6
And I said, Oh that I had wings like a dove! For then would I fly away, and be at rest.

In the small rural Smyrna Baptist Church, midway between Courtland and Moulton, Alabama, a trio rose to sing a song that was literally sweeping the South. The year was 1948, and the occasion was the funeral of my grandfather, James Terry. The song was written just seventeen years before, by one of our nation's leading gospel songwriters, Albert E. Brumley. It is one of more than six hundred songs that seemed to flow from his pen.

That unique song "I'll Fly Away," has been played and sung in some of the nation's largest auditoriums and by one of our country's most popular symphony orchestras. More than a hundred of Brumley's songs have been recorded by countless singers for major music companies. He is the only gospel song-writer to have four exclusive albums of his songs recorded on major labels.

Albert Brumley's rural background made it natural for him

to appeal to the common man. Even as a small lad picking cotton in LeFlore County, Oklahoma, he knew he would much rather be involved in music than in any other line of work. At age seventeen he began his serious music study, and in the next several years he received training and instruction from such notable men as Homer Rodeheaver, Virgil Stamps, and E. M. Bartlett, who wrote "Victory in Jesus."

In 1931, while teaching a singing school in Powell, Missouri, Brumley met and married Goldie Edith Schell. He had already begun his songwriting, but had done nothing with the songs. Goldie encouraged him to send his songs to a publisher, assuring him that they were good and that "any publisher would be glad to publish them."

One of the first songs submitted was "I'll Fly Away." This song, written during the depression, was carried by radio to the nation, along with many of Brumley's other songs. People everywhere were receiving renewed hope as they listened to such songs as "Turn Your Radio On," "I'll Meet You in the Morning," "Jesus, Hold My Hand," and, of course, "I'll Fly Away."

It has often been said that Albert Brumley's songs have been used in more places, by more people, than any other writer's. I am especially glad that he wrote:

> Some glad morning when this life is o'er, I'll fly away;
> To a home on God's celestial shore, I'll fly away.

> Just a few more weary days and then, I'll fly away;
> To a land where joys shall never end, I'll fly away.

> *Chorus*:
> I'll fly away, O glory, I'll fly away.
> When I die, Hallelujah, by and by,
> I'll fly away.

Reflection: Psalm 139:9a, 10: *If I take the wings of the morning . . . Even there shall thy hand lead me, and thy right hand shall hold me.*

40

A Moment of Truth

Song: *Greater Is He That Is in Me*
Scripture: 1 John 4:1–6
Ye are of God, little children, and have overcome them: because greater is he that is in you, than he that is in the world.

Lanny Wolfe, born on February 2, 1942, is probably the most-educated songwriter of Christendom today. He holds four degrees, two Bachelor's and two Master's from such schools as Ohio State University, San Jose State University, and Southern Illinois University. He has written approximately three hundred songs, most of them published.

This songwriter from Mississippi is presently involved in music at Jackson College of Ministries. He is also the music director of a church in that city. He confesses that although his first two degrees were in another direction, a Bachelor of Science degree in business education and a master's degree in business administration, he still had music in his "gut." He wanted to be involved with music, but had no background, which led him to the Western Apostolic Bible College in California for one year, before entering San Jose State.

Lanny says of his most famous song, "Greater Is He That Is in Me," that it came in response to a "moment of truth." He says, "I had read that Scripture many times [1 John 4:4], but it wasn't special until a certain time when I was riding in a car, traveling through Nevada, while going up to Montana. It was a moment when that Scripture, as I thought of it, became so real—the amazing fact that Christ lives within us and that he is so much more powerful and greater than the one who rules the affairs of the unsaved people of this world. Imagine—he lives within us and he is omnipotent!

"During those times I never wrote out songs. I just kept them in my head. Our singing group would then learn a song by having me sing it to them in a studio situation. It would then be written down so that it might be published. During those studio sessions, we are able to hone it and make what corrections seem necessary. That happened with "Greater Is He That Is in Me," and that is how the song came into being."

Hear again those wonderful words of affirmation:

> Greater is He that is in me,
> Greater is He that is in me,
> Greater is He that is in me
> Than he that is in the world.
>
> Satan's like a roaring lion, roaming to and fro,
> Seeking whom he may devour—the Bible tells us so.
> Many souls have been his prey to fall in some weak hour:
> But God has promised us today His overcoming power.
>
> On the day of Pentecost, a rushing mighty wind
> Blew into the upper room and baptized all of them
> With a power greater than any earthly foe;
> And I'm so glad I've got it too—
>   I'm gonna let the whole world know.

Reflection: What a marvelous existence we enjoy as children of God. Our Lord, with all of his omnipotence and his glory, actually dwells within our hearts. What protection, what security, and what joy!

41

It Came
Like a Dayspring

Song: *Surely the Presence of the Lord Is in This Place*
Scripture: Psalm 100
*Serve the LORD with gladness: come before his presence with
singing.*

Many songwriters have revealed that they occasionally
wrote songs in a very spontaneous fashion, but none that I
have interviewed have had the experience afforded Lanny
Wolfe one day in Columbia, Mississippi. He had gone there
with his singing ensemble to participate in the dedication service for a new church auditorium. Wolfe relates his experience:

> We were there to be a part of the festivities for the dedica-
> tion of the new building. The mayor of the city was there with
> all of the officials. The newness of the building was apparent.
> Everyone was proper and in place. It was everything you
> would expect at a church dedication.
> Before our trio got up to sing, the Lord dropped a tune and
> some lyrics in my mind. What was really strange about the situ-
> ation is that the music went in a certain progression that I

would not ordinarily go to, especially not being at a keyboard. But I'm sitting there and the Lord gives me this whole chorus. So, when it was time for the trio to sing, I stepped to the piano and sang through the chorus, just as the Lord gave it. I taught it to the audience and at the same time, Marietta, my wife, and Dave, who sings with us, learned it.

Lanny sang the song through completely as it came — like a dayspring. It has never been changed. Now, all over the world, people sing the chorus:

> Surely the Presence of the Lord is in this place,
> I can feel His mighty power and His grace;
> I can feel the brush of angel's wings,
> I see Glory on each face.
> Surely the Presence of the Lord is in this place.

The original scrap of paper on which Lanny Wolfe scribbled a few notes during that service now hangs, framed, in the vestibule of that church.

Reflection: The omnipresence of our Savior gives us the calm assurance that his glory is our satisfaction and our joy as we serve him with gladness.

42

The Lord
Gave Him the Song

Song: *More Than Wonderful*

Scripture: Isaiah 9:1–7

For unto us a child is born, unto us a son is given: and the government shall be upon his shoulder: and his name shall be called Wonderful, Counselor, The mighty God, The everlasting Father, The Prince of Peace.

The music publishers almost talked Lanny Wolfe out of including in his new Christmas musical what eventually became the 1984 Song of the Year. Consider this strange story as Lanny Wolfe told it to me:

> We were going to work on a "second coming" musical. I had enough songs for two musicals. I went into a committee meeting with people from Benson Publishing Company in Nashville. It was a strange meeting. They said, "We don't think the marketplace is ready for a 'second coming' musical." The members of the committee were not excited about the Lord's return. I became discouraged as the men talked me out of the musical about Christ's return and persuaded me to do a

Christmas cantata. During one of the committee meetings, it was decided that we needed a song built around Isaiah 9:6: "Thou shalt call his name Wonderful."

I decided to call the Christmas work *Thou Shalt Call His Name Jesus*. So, I left the meeting and in the following days the Lord gave me a song, "More Than Wonderful." Our trio started singing the song in church services, and we got a marvelous response.

I went back to the committee meeting and said, "I have this song that the Lord gave me, based on Isaiah 9:6." Bob McKenzie, an official of the Benson Company at the time, said, "You know, Lanny, I think you can write a better song. I don't think we should put this in this Christmas musical."

I went away very discouraged. I *know* when an audience is responding to a song, and they have responded greatly to that one. At later meetings I argued with Bob McKenzie about putting the song in the musical. We did so against his wishes.

I suggested that we have Larnelle Harris and Sandi Patti sing the song as a duet on the demonstration tape. Because of the acceptance of that duet, the song became Song of the Year in 1984, Sandi Patti was named female vocalist of the year, Sandi Patti and Larnelle Harris received Grammy Awards for their performance, and I was named Songwriter of the Year.

The marvelous lyrics of that song are:

He promised us that He would be a Counselor,
A Mighty God and a Prince of Peace;
He promised us that He would be a Father,
And would love us with a love that would not cease.

Well, I tried Him and I found His promises are true;
He's everything He said that He would be.
The finest words I know could not begin to tell
Just how much Jesus really means to me.

For He's more wonderful than my mind can conceive,
He's more wonderful than my heart can believe,
He goes beyond my highest hopes and fondest dreams.
He's everything that my soul ever longed for,
Everything He's promised and so much more.

More than amazing, more than marvelous,
More than miraculous could ever be.
He's more than wonderful;
That's what Jesus is to me.

I stand amazed to think the King of Glory
Would come to live within the heart of man.
I marvel just to know He really loves me,
When I think of who He is and who I am.

I am glad that Lanny Wolfe stood his ground and insisted that the song the Lord gave to him be passed on to you and me. It is a mighty instrument in the lifting of praise to the Savior.

Reflection: Not even a small fraction of his glory and his majesty can be imagined by us who are finite. The infinite wonder of his person defies our description.

43

They Wept
as They Sang

Song: *One Day Too Late*
Scripture: Luke 21:25–38
And all the people came early in the morning to him in the temple, for to hear him.

From Northside Baptist Church in Charlotte, North Carolina, a group of teenage singers and I traveled to the tiny island country of Haiti. What a needy place! What needy people! Our mission was to be of encouragement to the missionary, to give out Christian literature, and to preach the Word.

On a bright, sunshiny Sunday morning the young people stood in the little dirt-floor mission church and sang to a house filled to capacity. There were people by the score standing outside, looking in the windows, doors, or wherever they could get a glance of the happenings inside.

As the teens stood before those hungry people, they began to weep and sing, "One Day Too Late." It was one of the most meaningful Christian experiences of my life.

You can imagine how I felt when Lanny Wolfe, the com-

poser, offered to tell me how he came to write this song. He
said, "We were on our way from Jackson, Mississippi, to a
church in Arlington, Texas, to sing in a concert. The pastor
who had picked up our trio at the Dallas Airport, during some
conversation as we rode along, used the phrase 'one day too
late.' It struck a responsive chord in my heart, and the beginning of a new song was eminent."

That song has been a blessing to many thousands across our
nation. Blessings on Lanny Wolfe for writing these words:

> I never thought I'd see the day when you'd come to kneel and
>   pray;
> I never thought that I would see the church house filled to
>   capacity;
> And outside the door there's more who have never come
>   before;
> Oh, what a shame that Jesus came one day before!

> You tried to live the best you could, tried to do the things you
>   should;
> But when it came to serving God, you said, "I still have time
>   to wait";
> But now it's all turned around, time to serve Him now you've
>   found;
> How sad the fate: you found the time one day too late!

> *Chorus*:
> You came just one day too late, one day too late!
> Jesus came, and you've been left behind to wait!
> Yesterday you couldn't find time for Jesus on your mind;
> You finally came to call His name, but one day too late!

The Lord has used this song to speak to thousands of people
in many places. The urgency of the lyrics is a soul-stirring challenge—a call to do what we must for Christ, *today!*

Lanny Wolfe will, God willing, do many more wonderful
things, but none more effective than the writing of this song.

Reflection: May the realization of the message of this song
drive us to reaching out to a lost world before it is too late.

44

Human Struggle Inspires a Song

Song: *Learning to Lean*

Scripture: 2 Corinthians 12:7–10

And he said unto me, My grace is sufficient for thee: for my strength is made perfect in weakness.

John Stallings, a Georgia native from the small town of Griffin, near Atlanta, was only sixteen years of age when he began his songwriting career. He has had almost half of his more than 250 songs published. He is a self-taught musician who travels around the country as a singing evangelist.

At age thirty-four, while pastoring a church in Montgomery, Alabama, Stallings's serene little world began to tumble down around him. One of his three daughters nearly died with a serious illness, another was almost killed in an automobile accident. During this time, he felt the need to resign from his Alabama pastorate, and he moved to Florida. His furniture had to be stored in three different places. Stallings was trying to construct a home, but things were not going well at all. He knew he was going to have to learn to live by the faith about which he has preached for many years.

In the midst of all these struggles, a song title began rolling around in his mind. So, one day he sat down in the living room of the place where he lived at the time, and wrote this now-familiar chorus:

> I'm learning to lean, learning to lean,
> Learning to lean on Jesus.
> Finding more power than I'd ever dreamed;
> I'm learning to lean on Jesus.

Stallings began to sing the chorus in some of his services, as an "altar service" song. Much to his surprise, while in a church in Cape Girardeau, Missouri, the pastor, after hearing the chorus, published it in his church bulletin. People began to sing the song and to ask about it.

After writing the chorus, Stallings had thought very little about it because, in his words, "It came so easily." Now he thought, "Well, if they like the chorus so much, then I'll try to write some verses to go with it." And he did so, about six or eight months following the writing of the chorus. That was in 1975. The rest is history. The song began to sweep the country and has been a perennial favorite for all these years since.

Stallings tells of one lady who was so bent on destroying herself that she actually held a gun to her head. Suddenly from another room she heard the heartwarming strains of "Learning to Lean." She put the gun aside and now credits this song with saving her from suicide.

A man who is now pastoring a church in Louisiana became a Christian because he heard a traveling musical group sing the song. And a number of pastors have testified that the hearing of that song helped them through low valleys in their ministries, causing them to keep on for the Lord. It is the only song that has ever won all three of the major sacred-song awards in the same year (1977): The Dove Award, The Singing News Award, and The Quartet Convention Award.

Blessings on John Stallings for allowing the Lord to use him and for giving to all of us this song:

A joy I can't explain is filling my soul
Since the day I met Jesus my King;
His blessed Holy Spirit is leading my way;
He is teaching, and I'm learning to lean.

There's glorious vict'ry each day now for me
As I dwell in His peace so serene;
He helps me with each task if only I ask,
Ev'ry day now I am learning to lean.

Chorus:
I'm learning to lean, learning to lean,
Learning to lean on Jesus.
Finding more power than I'd ever dreamed;
I'm learning to lean on Jesus.

Reflection: When we have come to the end of our endurance, the Lord's strength in us has only begun. We need only to lean on him to be empowered in our weakness.

45

Left in God's Hands

Song: *God Will Take Care of You*
Scripture: Psalm 121
The LORD is thy keeper: the LORD is thy shade upon thy right hand.

"Daddy, you go on to the meetings. God will take care of us!" was the startling reply of William Stillman Martin's young daughter one day in 1905. Martin, an itinerant evangelist, had hesitated to leave home on this particular journey because of the illness of his wife. The Martins then lived on the campus of Bible School Park in Binghamton, New York, one of the first Bible institutes in America.

William Martin was instrumental in getting Will Houghton into a full-time Christian vocation. Houghton later became pastor of two famous churches, Baptist Tabernacle in Atlanta, Georgia, and Calvary Baptist Church in New York City. He also became president of Moody Bible Institute in Chicago.

It was at the little home in Binghamton that our story took place. Martin had been booked in some meetings and was about to leave when his wife became ill. He was so concerned with her well-being that he was on the verge of canceling the services to stay home with her, when his daughter made her surprising statement. He took that as God's words of assurance, and proceeded to go to his appointments.

When Martin arrived at his destination, he called back home and found that his wife was fully recovered. The Lord truly had taken care of her. Inspired by the incident and in grateful appreciation and thanksgiving, she wrote a beautiful poem. It began:

> Be not dismayed whate'er betide,
> God will take care of you!
> Beneath His wings of love abide,
> God will take care of you!
>
> *Chorus*:
> God will take care of you,
> Through every day, o'er all the way;
> He will take care of you;
> God will take care of you!

When her husband returned, Mrs. Martin recounted the story behind her poem to him, and he wrote a musical setting that has helped carry it into many a troubled heart to reassure and remind of the Lord's omnipotent watchcare over his children.

Reflection: Sometimes we may forget that God is watching over us, but he never forgets, not for a second. He sees and he knows and he cares for you, all the time and all the way.

46

Of Infinite Worth

Song: *His Eye Is on the Sparrow*

Scripture: Matthew 10:28–42

Are not two sparrows sold for a farthing? and one of them shall not fall on the ground without your Father. . . . Fear ye not therefore, ye are of more value than many sparrows.

A severe state of depression had overtaken a friend of Mrs. William Stillman Martin. She lived about thirty-five miles away, in Elmira, New York. It seemed that her life was a shambles as she passed through some very deep waters. It is always good to have a true friend to lean on in just such a time, and Mrs. Martin was such a friend. A few months earlier Mrs. Martin had experienced the protecting hand of the Lord during an illness. The incident was so overwhelmingly precious to her that it prompted her to write a song, "God Will Take Care of You," as we have seen in the previous story.

She proceeded to relate that story to her despondent friend, hoping in some way to help relieve her depressed state. After hearing the story, the friend said, "You know, I shouldn't worry, should I? We are promised in the Bible that God watches over the little sparrows." Mrs. Martin agreed, "He surely does." They then had a little time of rejoicing over God's wonderful watchcare and protection.

The journey back home was made shorter for Mrs. Martin by the satisfying realization that she had helped her friend. When she arrived home, she sat down and penned the words to one of the most beautiful and famous of all the gospel songs:

> Why should I feel discouraged?
> Why should the shadows come?
> Why should my heart be lonely,
> And long for heav'n and home,
> When Jesus is my portion?
> My constant Friend is He;
> His eye is on the sparrow,
> And I know He watches me,
> His eye is on the sparrow,
> And I know He watches me.

> *Chorus*:
> I sing because I'm happy,
> I sing because I'm free;
> For His eye is on the sparrow,
> And I know He watches me.

Charles H. Gabriel, another famous songwriter, set this beautiful poem to music. It has been made famous, perhaps more than by any other person, by Ethel Waters, as she sang it during the Billy Graham Crusades and on national television.

Reflection: None of us would ever fret or worry over a single problem if we would remember that the heavenly Father cares more for his human children than for all of his other earthly creatures. He cares more for you than you care for yourself.

47

Longing for Something to Sing

Song: *When the Roll Is Called Up Yonder*
Scripture: Deuteronomy 28:1–14
The Lord shall open unto thee his good treasure, the heaven to give the rain unto thy land in his season, and to bless all the work of thine hand: and thou shalt lend unto many nations, and thou shalt not borrow.

James M. Black was a Sunday school teacher and president of the young people's society in a church in Canada. He was quite young himself at the time. One day he met a girl, fourteen years of age, poorly clothed and the child of a drunkard. It was evident that she did not enjoy the nicer things of life that many teenagers enjoyed. Young Black was moved to invite her to attend Sunday school and to join the young people's group. He thought this would be a great blessing and help to her, and might even win her to Christ.

One evening at a consecration meeting, when each member answered the roll call by repeating a Scripture text, the girl failed to respond. This situation brought the thought to Black's mind that it would be a very sad thing if our names are called

from the Lamb's Book of Life in heaven and we should be
absent. The thought, although not theologically sound, brought
this prayer to the lips of Black: "Oh, God, when my name is
called up yonder, may I be there to respond!"

He then longed for something suitable to sing, but found
nothing in the books at hand. He closed the meeting that night
and, while on his way home, was still wishing that there might
be a song that could be sung on such an occasion. All of a sudden the thought came: "Why don't you write it?" He tried to
dismiss the idea, thinking that he could never write such a
song.

When Black reached his house, his wife saw that he was
deeply troubled and questioned him about his problem, but he
did not reply. He only thought of the song that he would like to
write. All of a sudden, like a dayspring from on high, the first
stanza came in full. He later said that in fifteen minutes he had
composed the other two verses. He then went to the piano and
played the music just as you will find it in the hymnbooks
today—note for note. It has never been changed.

Try to sing the verses. I am sure you know the melody,
because you have heard it many times before:

> When the trumpet of the Lord shall sound and time
>   shall be no more,
> When the morning breaks; eternal, bright and fair;
> When the saved of earth shall gather over on the other
>   shore,
> And the roll is called up yonder, I'll be there.
>
> When the roll is called up yonder,
> When the roll is called up yonder,
> When the roll is called up yonder,
> When the roll is called up yonder,
>   I'll be there.

James M. Black was born in Scotland on February 22,
1882. He was kidnapped at the age of eight and brought to
Canada, where he was found by an aged minister and taken to
the minister's home. It was not until he was seventeen years of

age, that he returned to his native Scotland and was reunited with his father and began to be active in Christian service.

Sometime later he returned to America. While on board the ship, on the way over, he heard the news that his home had been burned. Out of this experience came his other beautiful song, "Where Jesus Is 'Tis Heaven There." He died in an auto accident in Colorado in 1948 but will always be remembered for his songs, most especially for "When the Roll Is Called Up Yonder."

Reflection: God can preserve the life of a kidnapped lad, bring him into circumstances that would lead him to a saving knowledge of Christ and make him a blessing by causing him to write a song that rings around the world in many languages. Surrendered, you can be of great service to God, too—perhaps not in that way, but in his way and his time and according to the gifts he has given you.

48

The Sunshine Within

Song: *Summertime in My Heart*

Scripture: Psalm 32

Be glad in the LORD, and rejoice, ye righteous: and shout for joy, all ye that are upright in heart.

It was very cold in Minneapolis, Minnesota, that night in January 1940. The ground was covered with snow, with more falling. Lois Johnson was snugly in bed at her home. The young woman didn't like the bleakness or the cold of the winter night, but because she was a Christian she had God's sunshine flooding her heart. In fact, she thought to herself, "It is always summertime in the hearts of those who have Christ dwelling within."

Suddenly a melody began to run through her mind, and with it came these words:

> It is summertime in my heart,
> It is summertime in my heart,
> Since Jesus saved me, new life He gave me,
> Even in wintertime, it's summer in my heart.

On waking the next morning Lois Johnson's thoughts immediately turned to the melody and verse born the night before. She hurried to the piano and began to play and sing the newborn song. She then put it on paper, taking only about ten or fifteen minutes to do so.

Harry Clark came to her home the next day and heard her play and sing it. That same evening he had her play and sing it for the congregation where he was preaching in a series of revival services. It was taught to the congregation that same evening, and they sang it heartily. A few weeks later, Clark published it in a booklet of songs. Thus began the life of the increasingly popular chorus, "Summertime in My Heart," which is now published by Singspiration.

Lois Johnson was born in Minneapolis, where she studied piano and voice at the McPhail School of Music. In 1943 she became the wife of Harvey John Fritsch, who is presently the pastor of Community Christian Church in Miami, Florida.

"Summertime in My Heart" has been translated into at least two foreign languages. It has been heard nationally on television, as sung by a famous women's quartet. It was later recorded by the same quartet in a medley of choruses. The album in which it can be heard has sold more than a quarter of a million copies.

The zenith of Lois Johnson Fritsch's musical ambitions for the Lord was accomplished when she was chosen to play the organ for the Billy Graham Crusade in Miami in 1961. She accompanied the meetings for a week of the crusade.

As you attend the Youth for Christ rallies or evangelistic services across the United States, or even as you walk the streets of the mountain towns of Colombia, South America, you will be thrilled when you hear happy voices singing, "Summertime in My Heart."

Reflection: The summertime is a time of bright sunshine, happy outdoor games, and fellowship. Spiritually, this should describe our hearts—full of thanksgiving, love, and goodwill. We should be enjoying the pleasures of being a Christian every day of our lives.

49

Too Good to Be True?

Song: *Some Golden Daybreak*
Scripture: 1 Thessalonians 4:9–18
For the Lord himself shall descend from heaven with a shout, with the voice of the archangel, and with the trump of God; and the dead in Christ shall rise first.

Some years ago, while preaching on the radio on the subject of the rapture, the glorious hope of all Christians, the Rev. C. A. Blackmore was outlining some of the marvelous things that would happen to Christians on that wonderful day. He declared that deformities and pains will vanish as they leave this old body of clay and instantaneously take on a glorified spiritual form.

A lady who had been bedridden for twenty-three years heard the message. To her it seemed too good to be true. She wrote to Blackmore inquiring: "Will I really be well? Will all pain and sorrow actually be gone?" Blackmore replied: "Yes, my friend, some glorious day, when Jesus comes, you will leap from that bed with all the vigor of a youth and never know pain again. Little cripples will be made perfect, with no more crying and no more heartaches. All will be peace."

Blackmore's son, Carl, who had already become widely known for his musical achievements, was greatly impressed with the reality of this coming event. As he pondered the glorious prospects, the words and melody of a chorus took form in his mind. Simultaneously, a melody for some verses was likewise inspired, and he said to his father: "Dad, you should write some verses for this chorus." They agreed to ask the Lord to give the inspiration and guidance. After much prayer and meditation, early one morning, unable to sleep as he anticipated the thrill of the rapture, the elder Blackmore rose from his bed and wrote the verses as they remain today.

As the song became known, it grew in popularity, until today it is used by all the leading publishers of gospel songs in this country and abroad. It has also been recorded by one of the nation's outstanding orchestra conductors. Here is a portion of that song, best known as "Some Golden Daybreak":

> Some glorious morning, sorrow will cease;
> Some glorious morning, all will be peace;
> Heartaches all ended, labor all done,
> Heaven will open, Jesus will come.

> *Chorus:*
> Some golden daybreak, Jesus will come;
> Some golden daybreak, battles all won;
> He'll shout the vict'ry, break through the blue;
> Some golden daybreak, for me, for you.

Reflection: There is nothing more beautiful than the sunrise, the time when men feel farthest from the darkness. That is another reminder of heaven. When we stand in the brightness of Christ, the light of the universe, it truly will be a glorious morning—a golden daybreak.

50

No Better Friend

Song: *No One Ever Cared for Me Like Jesus*

Scripture: Psalm 28

The LORD is my strength and my shield; my heart trusted in him, and I am helped; therefore, my heart greatly rejoiceth; and with my song will I praise him.

"Let 'er rip!" was an expression of one of America's foremost gospel song writers, Dr. Charles F. Weigle. These little words, odd as they may seem, simply suggest that you need not worry about situations over which you have little or no control. "Leave it in the hands of God" is the godly attitude that caused Dr. Weigle to be a blessing and inspiration to countless thousands of people during his fruitful life. His life of service to God has been enhanced greatly by his ability to write gospel songs.

Dr. Weigle was not without his hours of trouble and heartache. Yet, it seems that out of these grievous sorrows flowed forth one of the most beautiful and widely known songs, "No One Ever Cared for Me Like Jesus." Phil Kerr reported that among gospel singers, radio soloists, and broadcasters, several said that requests for this song outnumbered those for any other special gospel song. It has been sung around the world and has been translated into many languages. Yet, this song of grateful confidence was born out of despair.

One night, while going through a period of great stress of soul, brought on by a domestic problem, Dr. Weigle sat down at the piano with this thought in mind: "Jesus knows all about us and he truly cares for us more than any other." He had a short time earlier walked down to the pier near his home and had for a few faltering seconds thought that he could end his personal torment by jumping into the Gulf of Mexico. Something had stopped him. Now, back at the house, his hands fell on the keys and he began to play and sing. In about twenty minutes a great song was born.

Numerous stories could be written about the music of Charles Weigle. In all, he has written more than four hundred songs; several have become very popular among Christians everywhere, perhaps none more beloved than this one:

> I would love to tell you what I think of Jesus.
> Since I found in Him a friend so strong and true;
> I would tell you how He changed my life completely,
> He did something that no other friend could do.
>
> No one ever cared for me like Jesus,
> There's no other friend so kind as He;
> No one else could take the sin and darkness from me,
> O, how much He cared for me.

Some of our greatest hymns were written out of times of deep distress and darkness on the part of their writers. Perhaps during such periods a suffering soul draws closer to God and is able to draw tremendous spiritual inspiration from these times of intimacy. The same can be true in your life. Do not despise the valleys in your daily routine, because if it were not for the valleys, there would be no mountaintop experiences.

Reflection: When the night seems the darkest, hold on. It may be that God is getting you ready to be used of him. We become most acutely aware of his power and presence when we call on him in times of great distress and sorrow.

51

Comfort and Refuge

Song: *I Have Found a Hiding Place*
Scripture: Psalm 91
He that dwelleth in the secret place of the Most High shall abide under the shadow of the Almighty.

Not long ago it was my privilege to direct the music for a great evangelist and songwriter, Dr. Charles Weigle. The unusual power with which this preacher exhorted the people is seldom witnessed in our modern day. It was refreshing to my soul to see men weeping their way into the arms of Jesus.

During the afternoon of one of those days, I spent a couple of hours in interview with Dr. Weigle, gathering from him some details of his rich experiences in writing such songs as "No One Ever Cared For Me Like Jesus" and "I Have Found A Hiding Place." (This article is written about the latter.)

It was in 1942, as Dr. Weigle sat on his front porch in Sebring, Florida, that he decided to write a song that used some of the titles given to Christ in the Bible. At first he wrote only a chorus and later sang it for a friend. This friend urged him to put verses to it because of its singable quality.

So many of the titles or names given to Christ in the Bible

159

are descriptive of his powers or his character. Some of them describe his saving ability, some his power to comfort and heal. Others tell about his lovingkindness, while still others emphasize his exalted position with the Father. (Can you think of some different titles given to Christ not mentioned in this devotion?)

Dr. Weigle took the suggestion of his friend and began to write. For the theme of one stanza he chose one biblical title of our Savior: "Rose of Sharon."

> I have found the sweetest flower that ever grew,
> Jesus, "Rose of Sharon," fair and pure.
> He's my joy and comfort, blessed Friend so true,
> He blooms within my heart evermore.

For another stanza of "I Have Found a Hiding Place," Weigle took the title "Rock of Ages."

> I have found a hiding place when sore distressed.
> Jesus, "Rock of Ages," strong and true;
> In a weary land I in His shadow rest,
> He is my strength in all that I do.

Now read with adoration in your heart that soul-stirring chorus that started this song on its mission for the Savior:

> Jesus, "Rock of Ages," let me hide in Thee.
> Jesus, "Rose of Sharon," sweet Thou art to me;
> "Lily of the Valley," "Bright and Morning Star,"
> Fairest of ten thousand to my soul.

Dr. Weigle has written over four hundred gospel songs and hymns. For sixty-seven years of evangelism, he burned with zeal for God.

Reflection: One of the most wonderful aspects of Christianity is that one can find refuge, even in times like these, under the sheltering arms of a loving, heavenly Father, through his Son—the "Rock of Ages" and hiding place.

52

His Own Song
Led Him to Christ

Song: *Ten Thousand Angels*
Scripture: Matthew 26:47–56
Thinkest thou that I cannot now pray to my Father, and he shall presently give me more than twelve legions of angels?

Rarely in the history of hymnology has a composer been led to Christ by his own song, but such was the case with Ray Overholt. God literally picked him up out of the darkness and confusion of the nightclubs and brought him under his loving care, using his song in an unusual manner.

Ray Overholt was born in Middleville, Ohio, in 1924. He seemed destined to a career in music from age eleven, when his dad gave him his first guitar. He rose to a measure of success, hosting his own television show and appearing on Kate Smith's national program.

In 1958, then thirty-six and at the height of his show-business career, Ray Overholt wrote his now-famous song, "Ten Thousand Angels." Here is his story as he related it to me:

I had left my television show, "Ray's Roundup" and entered the nightclub circuit. I was drinking pretty heavily at this time. I began thinking that there must be a better life than the nightclub, show-business whirlwind. I was so intent on changing my lifestyle that I went home and told my wife that I was quitting all of the smoking, drinking, and cursing. I wanted to clean up my own life. Why I was doing all of this I didn't know, but I knew there were people praying for me.

One day I thought, *I've written secular songs: I'd like to write a song about Christ.* I opened the Bible, which I very seldom read. I knew a little about it from my mom. I began to read the portion of Scripture that describes Jesus in the Garden of Gethsemane, telling Peter to put away his sword. I read where Jesus told Peter that he could ask his Father and he would send twelve legions of angels. I didn't know at the time that that would have been more than 72,000 angels.

I thought a good title for a song would be "He Could Have Called Ten Thousand Angels." I didn't know what had happened during the life of Christ, so I began doing a little research. The more I read about Jesus, the more I admired him for what he had done. I then remembered that he did this all for me, also.

I was playing in a nightclub in Battle Creek, Michigan, when the Lord impressed me to write the song. I wrote the first verse and put it in my guitar case. I then gave the club my notice that I was quitting. As I opened my guitar case to put my instrument away, one of the fellows saw the music written out and he asked, "What are you doing there?" I told him I was writing a song about Jesus. He asked the title and I told him. He said, "It will never go." I asked, "Why not?" He said, "I don't even like the title." But I finished the song and sent it to a publishing house, which reluctantly agreed to publish it.

Sometime later I found myself singing at a small church. I sang "He Could Have Called Ten Thousand Angels." Following my singing, a preacher spoke a message that gripped my heart. I knew I needed Christ, so I knelt there and accepted, as my Savior, the One whom I had been singing and writing about.

Ray Overholt became a traveling singer and preacher. He has written a number of other songs, but none so moving as "Ten Thousand Angels."

They bound the hands of Jesus in the garden where
    He prayed
They led Him through the streets in shame.
They spat upon the Savior, so pure and free from sin
They said, "Crucify Him, He's to blame."

To the howling mob He yielded; He did not for mercy
    cry.
The cross of shame He took alone.
And when He cried, "It's finished," He gave Himself
    to die;
Salvation's wondrous plan was done.

Chorus:
He could have called ten thousand angels
To destroy the world and set Him free.
He could have called ten thousand angels
But He died alone for you and me.

Reflection: Before we knew him, God loved us. And so he drew us to himself through his Son and set us free.

53

The Source of Inspiration

Song: *Unworthy*
Scripture: John 3:22–36
He must increase, but I must decrease.

"I read *Worthy Is He,* and all these tremendous personal convictions overwhelmed me. Our Lord is the only one to whom we should give ourselves." Those are words of Gloria Roe. She had been confined to a hospital and had "tried to do as much reading as I could, but I wasn't even interested in reading the magazines or books that were brought to me, just reading my Bible," she adds.

This gifted pianist and prolific writer of gospel music was born in Pasadena, California. Her parents were Mennonites from Germany, and their daughter was raised in a very religious home. She gave her heart to the Lord as a Sunday school student, but she learned that it was one thing to give the Lord your heart and yet quite another to give him your life. She says, "I did not do that until my junior year in high school, when some girls tricked me into going to a youth rally."

Gloria studied piano at the Zoolowiniski School of Music in

Hollywood after being awarded a scholarship by the Screen Guild of Hollywood. She also attended Pasadena Nazarene College, after which she entered full-time Christian service, expecting to go to the mission field. At the time she did not really care about the musical aspect of Christian service, wanting only to do what the Lord had in mind for her.

As a college student, Miss Roe was not acquainted with evangelism or with gospel music as she knows it now, but was led into the Lord's work by Phil Kerr. She has since written more than three hundred gospel songs and has three songbooks and four volumes of piano arrangements to her credit, along with two Christmas cantatas. She often gives programs of sacred music in which she shares her testimony with the audience.

Here, in her own words, is the story of how one of Gloria Roe's most beautiful songs was born out of that long-ago hospital stay:

I had never had any aspirations along the line of writing or creating anything original, but one evening a gentleman and his wife, music director and youth leaders at the Church of God in El Cajon, California, called on me, knowing that I was ill. They tried to comfort me during those days of sickness. I shared with them the thoughts on my heart, how I had received from the Lord that day a new insight into the beauty of our salvation and our relationship with Christ. I told them that "there is only one pattern for living, based upon knowing Christ, and that is total commitment. Who are we to hold back anything from him?"

About a month later, I was in San Diego and attended some church services. After one of the services the same young couple came up to me and gave me a poem that they had been inspired to create as a result of our visit. The poem was called "I Am Not Worthy." I read it and appreciated it, so they left it with me. For the next couple of weeks I was still recuperating, and as I rested and relaxed, I continued to read the Scriptures. Various thoughts stuck with me. I studied in Hebrews where it says, "We should give more earnest heed to things that we have heard" and "How shall we escape if we neglect so great salvation?" Those thoughts haunted me. Before I knew it, I was putting down a set of words that I titled "So Great Salvation," which eventually rhymed. As I looked at it completed, I sang it as if it were a song—as if it were a song that I had always known.

I shared this with my closest friend in the ministry at that time, Bill Carl. He is now gone to be with the Lord. He said to me, "Do you know that in these days that you have been tried and tested, the Lord has given you an added ministry? Please write down everything that comes to you, because I believe that you are writing music."

I then began to refer back to the poem that the young couple had given me, entitled "I Am Not Worthy." This time with it came a melody, and as the melody came, it seemed that I should change it to "I Am Unworthy." It seemed that a new set of words just flowed from my mind:

> I am unworthy of the price He paid for me
> I am unworthy of His death on Calvary.
> I am unworthy to call upon His name,
> Yet He loved me,
> Still He loves me.

> I am unworthy of the blood He freely gave,
> I am unworthy for in sin I was a slave.
> I am unworthy that He should bear my shame,
> Yet He loved me,
> Still He loves me, Praise His Holy Name.

I closed the song with a verse of praise to the Lord for what he had done. It turned out to be a very simple progression, a very simple form of song, and the shortest form of song I have ever written. And yet I entitled it "Unworthy." I stay in the Word all the time; now that's my source of inspiration.

If you and I begin to realize the depths of God's love and think of all that our lives can mean to the cause of Christ when we serve him, we would with thanksgiving begin to reflect on our "unworthy" souls. Those great truths are etched forever in the same Book from which Gloria Roe learned so many valuable lessons and from which she gained so much inspiration for her life's journey.

Reflection: He has no eyes but our eyes, no voice but our voices, no feet but our feet, and we have no righteousness but his goodness, no melody but his song, no money but his great wealth, no purity but his sinlessness—and no worth but his worthiness.

54

Against All Human Odds

Song: *Nothing Is Impossible*
Scripture: Philippians 4:1–13
I can do all things through Christ which strengtheneth me.

Eugene L. Clark rose to be the personification of the title of his most famous song, "Nothing Is Impossible." Although his fingers once flew across the piano keyboard, he later became a victim of crippling arthritis. And eyes that could once seemingly read whole music scores at a single glance were now totally blind. But Eugene Clark, former music director and organist for the broadcast "Back to the Bible" never learned the meaning of the word *quit*.

Born in Maxwell, Nebraska, in 1925, young Clark began writing songs as a high-school lad. He later attended Moody Bible Institute, graduating in 1948. He was that school's alumnus-of-the-year in 1973, but was unable to attend the ceremonies because of confinement to bed.

It finally became impossible for Clark to continue playing the organ or piano, but when bedridden, never to get up again,

168

he requested that they bring to his bedside a dictating machine. With this marvelous electric invention and his most valuable possession, a keen mind, he continued to give to the world his beautiful musical offerings. His trust in the Lord became monumental.

Great odds did not stifle Eugene Clark's ability and desire to serve Christ and be a blessing to millions around the world. Hundreds of gospel songs and hymns, scores of choir arrangements, and three missionary cantatas have flowed through his dedicated heart and mind into the Christian world.

His best-known song, "Nothing Is Impossible," was introduced in 1964 and has sold more than one million copies. Ruth Johnson reports in the March 1973 issue of *Good News Broadcaster* that Clark spent much time thinking and praying as he "wrote" each musical composition and arrangement. A note, a rest, a bar, and a dot at a time, the machine has recorded the product of his active mind—something that neither total blindness nor crippling arthritis could conquer.

Clark was quick to credit his wife with a great deal of the success of his ministry. Her love, loyalty, and patience were invaluable assets to his work.

May his life and labor be an inspiration to you and me. May we, too, learn to keep going in the face of great odds. We must keep working for the Savior, as Eugene Clark always did.

Here is the great song that he wrote in affirmation of his faith:

> I read in the Bible the promise of God
> That nothing for Him is too hard.
> Impossible things He has promised to do
> If we faithfully trust in His Word.
>
> Nothing is impossible when you put your trust in God,
> Nothing is impossible when you're trusting in His
>   Word.
> Harken to the voice of God to thee:
> "Is there anything too hard for Me?"
> Then put your trust in God alone

And rest upon His Word;
For everything, O everything,
Yes, everything is possible — with God!

Reflection: Dear Lord, give me some of the courage and faith that you gave to Eugene Clark, to help me serve and trust you, no matter what! Through your power I am strong, and "nothing is impossible."

55

Welcoming Arms

Song: *Just As I Am*
Scripture: John 6:29–51
*All that the Father giveth me shall come to me; and him
that cometh to me I will in no wise cast out.*

Probably the most widely used song of consecration
today is "Just As I Am." It has been called the world's greatest
soulwinning hymn. Countless people have been influenced by
this song to give their hearts and lives to God. A complete volume could be written telling of the wonderful happenings in
connection with the singing of this one song.

Its author, Charlotte Elliott, suffered most of her life from
the ills of an invalid body. Many times her weakened condition
caused her great lamentation. Such was the case in 1836, when
her brother, H. V. Elliott, was raising funds for St. Mary's Hall
at Brighton, England, a college for the daughters of poor clergy-
men. She wanted to have some little part but was hindered by
reason of her infirmity. As she pondered how she could help
the cause, Charlotte decided to write a poem relevant to others
who were physically limited. She remembered the words of a

great preacher, Cesar Malon, who had talked to her fourteen years before. He had told her to come to Jesus, "just as you are," words that helped her to find Christ.

The resulting poem was published without Charlotte's name and was handed to her one day in leaflet form by her doctor, who did not realize that she was its author. Tears streamed down her face as she read the six verses and was told that copies of this poem were being sold and the money given to St. Mary's Hall. Miss Elliott then realized that she had at last made a significant contribution to the building of the school through the medium of her words of faith and humility:

> Just as I am, without one plea,
> But that Thy blood was shed for me,
> And that thou bidd'st me come to Thee,
> O Lamb of God, I come! I come!

> Just as I am, Thou wilt receive,
> Wilt welcome, pardon, cleanse, relieve,
> Because Thy promise I believe,
> O Lamb of God, I come! I come!

Only eternity will reveal the blessings heaped on other lives by this song. Charlotte Elliott probably would have shouted for joy, if she could have heard the following story. . . .

During a song service in a church, John B. Gough was asked by the man next to him in the pew what was to be sung. Physically, the questioner seemed a most pathetic sight—victim of a nervous disease that had left him blind and twisted in body. The poor man joined the congregation in the singing of the song "Just As I Am." As they came to the words, "Just as I am, poor, wretched, blind," the wretched creature lifted his sightless eyes to heaven and sang with his whole being. Gough later said, "I have heard the finest strains of an orchestra, a choir and a soloist this world can produce, but I had never heard music, until I heard that blind man sing 'O Lamb of God, I come, I come!'"

Reflection: "Because Thy promise I believe. . . ." Oh, that we could take God at his word! How thoroughly cleansed is the man who lets Christ wash him with his blood. Because God is our loving, heavenly Father, he makes it as easy as possible for us to be saved. It cost him all he had, but our part is simple—we need only reach out and he will accept us unconditionally.

56

The Joyful Homecoming

Song: *Tell Mother I'll Be There*

Scripture: Proverbs 22:1–19

Train up a child in the way he should go: and when he is old, he will not depart from it.

A saintly little woman in Canton, Ohio, who was affectionately known as "Mother McKinley," raised her children in the ways taught by the Lord, and each one of them received Christ as Savior at a very early age. As soon as they could walk, they strolled along with her to Sunday school each Sunday morning. Only one of her children became famous, and he became our national leader. His name was William McKinley. No one could have been more devoted to his mother than William. His Christ-like spirit was evident in his work, whether as a Sunday school teacher, Sunday school superintendent, lawyer, congressman, governor of Ohio, and finally President of the United States.

One report says that every day of William's life until his mother's death, he either wrote or telegraphed his mother if he was not able to see her. It is said that one day in 1897 President McKinley made his way from the White House to Canton by train, just to walk to church once more with his beloved mother. When she became ill that winter, he had a special telegraph wire connecting his mother's home in Ohio with the White House. It is also reported that he had a special train standing by ready to roll. One night when his mother's condition worsened and it looked like the end was near, her attendants wired the President and his return message came very soon: "Tell Mother I'll be there."

He rushed to her side and she breathed her last breath on December 12, 1897, in the arms of her son, President William McKinley, who was at that time fifty-four years of age. For more than an hour he did not move from her bedside.

A songwriter by the name of Charles M. Filmore was so inspired by this beautiful story that he wrote the wonderful and moving song "Tell Mother I'll Be There." Why don't you try to sing or speak these words with your family or as you sit there alone?

> When I was but a little child, how well I recollect,
> How I would grieve my mother with my folly and neglect,
> And now that she has gone to heav'n, I miss her tender care,
> O angels, tell my mother I'll be there.
>
> One day a message came to me, it bade me quickly come,
> If I would see my mother, ere the Savior took her Home;
> I promised her before she died, for heaven to prepare,
> O angels, tell my mother I'll be there.
>
> *Chorus*:
> Tell mother I'll be there in answer to her pray'r.
> This message, guardian angels, to her bear,
> Tell mother I'll be there, heav'n's joys with her to share,
> Yes, tell my darling mother I'll be there.

Reflection: To many people the sweetest word in the English language is "mother." Perhaps the greatest need today is for more godly parents to raise their children so that we might have more men like William McKinley, who never forgot the spiritual truths learned at his mother's knee. "Children, obey your parents in all things: for this is well pleasing unto the Lord" (Col. 3:20).

57

The Message Heard 'Round the World

Song: *Silent Night, Holy Night*
Scripture: Luke 2:1–12
For unto you is born this day in the city of David a Saviour, which is Christ the Lord.

In 1818 a band of roving actors appeared in the tiny village of Oberndorf, near Salzburg, a little valley town in the Austrian Alps. The showmen were there for the annual presentation of the Christmas story. It was to be held in St. Nicholas Church, but the organ was broken and could not be repaired in time. The crude show was presented in a private home, and the assistant pastor, Josef Mohr, was invited to attend. So impressed was he with the simplicity of the play and the sincerity of the actors that he began to reflect on the real meaning of the Christmas season.

Mohr strode to a hillside overlooking the village as it lay shrouded in a still, clear night. Words began to form in his mind—the verses of "Silent Night, Holy Night." He later presented the verses to the church organist, Franz Gruber, a schoolmaster and songwriter. It is reported that Gruber composed the musical setting the same day he received Mohr's poem.

On Christmas Eve that year, Gruber and Pastor Mohr sang the song to the little congregation gathered in the church. The organ was still in ill repair, forcing Gruber to accompany them on his guitar, which was still in existence as late as 1950.

This carol was a favorite from the beginning. Soon, Austrian concert singers, the Strasser Sisters, began singing it throughout Europe. From there it has orbited the earth again and again. It was translated into English from the Austrian language in 1863 by Jane Campbell and made its first appearance in America in 1871, in Charles Hutchins's *Sunday School Hymnal*.

"Silent Night, Holy Night" is one of those carols that "wears like steel." It is as fresh and beautiful today as the first time it was played and sung that Christmas Eve in a little Austrian town more than 170 years ago.

It is wonderful to have such a Savior, whose birthday is as much a time of rejoicing today as it was nearly two thousand years ago. We sing again and again, with joyful hearts, this simple tribute to his nativity:

> Silent night, holy night,
> All is calm, all is bright.
> Round yon Virgin Mother and Child
> Holy Infant, so tender and mild,
> Sleep in heavenly peace,
> Sleep in heavenly peace.

Reflection: Pause a few moments and be thankful for this wonderful gift of love from God the Father, who sent his only Son to be our Savior. Then, for you, too, it will be a silent, holy night!

58

The Day
the Cabinet Shop
Was Closed

Song: *The Solid Rock*

Scripture: Romans 5

Much more then, being now justified by his blood, we shall be saved from wrath through him.

Edward Mote rose from a heathenistic childhood to become a great writer and preacher. He said of his youth, "My Sundays were spent on the streets [of London] in play. So ignorant was I that I did not know there was a God."

Born in 1787, Mote eventually became a carpenter's apprentice and, through hard labor and conscientious efforts, came to own a cabinet shop. One day, while walking to his work, he began thinking that he should write a hymn. Before he reached his shop he had the chorus: "On Christ, the solid Rock, I stand. All other ground is sinking sand." Before the day ended he had added four stanzas.

The following Sunday, Mote visited in the home of a preacher friend whose wife was at the point of death. During the afternoon they read from the Scriptures and had prayer with her. Then, as the preacher looked for a hymnal to sing from, which was his custom, he could find none. Edward Mote reached into his pocket, pulled out his verses, and asked if they might be sung to her. And so they were. She seemed to enjoy them very much. Mote was so pleased that she found comfort in them that he had a thousand copies printed for distribution among his friends.

Some time later, Edward Mote became a Baptist preacher. His efforts made it possible for a house of worship to be built for his congregation. They were so grateful that they offered to deed the property to him, but he replied, "I do not want the chapel, I want only the pulpit; and when I cease to preach Christ, then turn me out of that." He served this congregation for more than twenty years, never missing a single Lord's Day for any cause.

In his seventy-seventh year, as he lay on his bed of sickness Mote said, "I think I am going to heaven, yes, I am nearing port. The truths I have preached I am now living upon, and they will do to die upon. Ah! The precious blood which takes away all our sins. It is this which makes peace with God."

What a victorious ending to a useful life! This man was reared in a godless home, learned an honorable trade, and gave it all up to become a preacher. His memory will remain for generations because he took time one day to write:

> My hope is built on nothing less
> Than Jesus' blood and righteousness.
> No merit of my own I claim
> But wholly lean on Jesus' name.
>
> *Chorus*:
> On Christ, the solid Rock, I stand.
> All other ground is sinking sand,
> All other ground is sinking sand.

Reflection: We trust the Lord and therefore we love him. Or we love him and therefore we trust him. Either way, Christ is a sure foundation.

59

An Important Request

Song: *Fill My Cup, Lord*

Scripture: John 4:5–29

The woman saith unto him, Sir, give me this water, that I might thirst not, neither come hither to draw.

The year was 1925. A young American woman gave birth to a son. This birth was special in that this child was born to medical missionaries in Chungking, China, and before he reached the age of fifty, he was to touch the lives of millions for God. His name was Richard Blanchard.

When Richard was less than five years of age, his parents were driven from China in the wake of a mighty Communist onslaught. The young couple and their child were brought to the United States and to the midwestern state of Indiana. As the child grew, he became tremendously interested in music, mainly the trombone. The late and great Homer Rodeheaver, because he was a friend of Richard's parents, paid fifty dollars for a down payment on such a horn, and the boy continued to make payments on it with revenues from a paper route.

The years ahead brought a hitch in the Navy for Richard, degrees from Mercer and Emory universities, and then a pastorate in the United Methodist Church. In the years that followed, he pastored several of the largest Methodist churches in the state of Florida.

Life was never to be a bed of roses for Richard Blanchard. A severe lung problem developed, and Blanchard was faced with two major operations that left him with only one-third of his lung capacity, but still an unswerving faith in God. A diminished physical well-being did not stop young Blanchard. In 1953, he embarked on a television ministry, "Horizons of Faith," seen on a Miami station for seven years. During this time he became the pastor of a church in Coral Gables, Florida.

It was while at that church that Blanchard was asked by a young couple to perform their marriage ceremony. He agreed to do so and had them come to his office for counseling sessions. When the time came for the second session, the couple was quite late for their appointment. Blanchard told his secretary, "I will wait for thirty minutes and I'm leaving," angered that they would be late for the session. He then went to a nearby Sunday school room and sat down to play the piano for a while. He later said, "When I was not in the mood to be used of God, God was in a mood to use me." In less than thirty minutes, as he waited for the young couple, God gave to him, like a flowing fountain, the beautiful and inspiring "Fill My Cup, Lord."

The song was first introduced to Bill Mann after a revival meeting in a layman's home in Fort Lauderdale, Florida. Blanchard played it for Mann to sing. Two years went by, and Mann finally recorded it on the Word record label in 1964. It has soared in popularity ever since. More than one hundred million copies of sheet music have been sold.

Bill Mann was once singing for a large crusade in England, in one of the largest concert halls, when someone approached him before one of the services and said, "The prime minister's wife, Mrs. Harold Wilson, would like to make a request. Would you sing a song for her?" Mann quickly agreed to do so, and her request was for "Fill My Cup, Lord."

I am sure that you have heard this song. Why don't you sing these words now?

> Like the woman at the well, I was seeking
> For things that could not satisfy.
> And then I heard my Savior speaking:
> "Draw from My well that never shall run dry."

> There are millions in this world who are craving
> The pleasures earthly things afford.
> But none can match the wondrous treasure
> That I find in Jesus Christ, my Lord.

> *Chorus*:
> Fill my cup, Lord, I lift it up, Lord!
> Come and quench this thirsting of my soul.
> Bread of Heaven, feed me till I want no more,
> Fill my cup, fill it up and make me whole!

As Richard Blanchard looks back over his life, he declares "even though God chose in his providence to impair my physical being, he has in so many other ways 'Filled My Cup.'"

Reflection: Have you been in a mood lately to be used of God? God is constantly ready to use you. Surrender to him completely today and he will quench your longings and direct your paths.

60

The Magnificent One

Song: *Majesty*

Scripture: Hebrews 1:1–14

*Who being the brightness of his glory, and the express
image of his person, and upholding all things by the word of
his power, when he had by himself purged our sins, sat down
on the right hand of the Majesty on high.*

Dr. Jack Hayford, pastor of the famous Church On
The Way in Van Nuys, California, is not only an outstanding
preacher and Bible teacher, but also a talented songwriter. His
most famous song, the composition that has brought him the
most acclaim, has a rather unusual history.

Several years ago, Dr. and Mrs. Hayford traveled for ten
days in Denmark, where he had speaking engagements.
Following their stay in Denmark, they took advantage of two
weeks of free time before another scheduled series of meetings,
a seminar in Oxford, England. It was to be a study of
"Spiritual Awakenings," under the direction of Dr. Edwin Orr.

The year was the silver anniversary of the coronation of
Elizabeth II as Queen of England. The celebrating, the countryside, and the spirit and enthusiasm of the English people,

coupled with the great historical significance of that kingdom, made those two weeks a very special time for the Hayfords. Dr. Hayford reports that he was completely caught up in the emotion of the occasion. As he walked among the people and saw them move about amid signs of history on every hand, he sensed a feeling of grandeur and nobility. While touring the countryside, stopping here and there to examine a significant bit of history, the couple made a short visit to Blenheim, the palace where Winston Churchill was born and raised and where he would occasionally go aside for a short rest during the horrors of World War II.

Although that war was a monumental chapter of history and a generation past, memories of those days and what had gone before came rushing back to Pastor Hayford. As he looked about he sensed, too, that even though individuals are greatly used in the course of man's existence on this earth, there is a greater power, the One who is the Author of our destiny.

As he felt the courage and motivation of the English people, Hayford realized that there was also a deep feeling in their hearts for the royalty who stood with them in dark hours. Even now they were excited about sharing in the celebration of their monarch. Suddenly there came to his mind a feeling that Christ wants his church to have such a sense of loyalty and fellowship, because he must be our leader in good times and bad.

As Hayford stood on the magnificent, well-groomed landscape surrounding Blenheim Palace, he said to his wife, "Honey, I can hardly describe to you all the things which this setting evokes in me. There is something of *majesty* in all this, and I believe it has a great deal to do with why people who lived here have been of such consequence in the shaping of history. I don't mean that buildings and beauty can beget greatness, but I do feel that some people fail to perceive their possibilities because of their dismal surroundings."

As he talked to her of how Christ wants to exercise his kingdom authority in our lives and our being, one word seemed to charge to the forefront: majesty! That word seemed at the moment to represent the glory, excellence, grace, and power of Christ. By comparison, Queen Elizabeth seemed but a paltry reminder of the royal heritage we enjoy as we worship the majesty of our risen Lord.

As the Hayfords pulled themselves from that regal place and drove away, Dr. Hayford said, "Take the notebook and write down some words, will you, Babe?" He then began to dictate the key, the notes, the timing, and the lyrics to one of the most popular new songs now being sung by Christians everywhere:

> Majesty, worship His Majesty!
> Unto Jesus be all glory, honor and praise.
> Majesty, Kingdom authority,
> Flows from His Throne, unto His own, His anthem raise.
> So exalt, lift up on high the Name of Jesus.
> Magnify, come glorify, Christ Jesus the King.
> Majesty, worship His Majesty.
> Jesus who died, now glorified, King of all kings.

The song was edited and completed some time later at the piano in the living room of their home. (Much of the information in this story was taken from Jack Hayford's book, *Worship His Majesty*, published by Word Publishing, Dallas, Texas.)

Reflection: When we see the great King and are face to face with his glory, it will be wonderful to forever adore his majesty and his power. While we wait, we bow to his authority as we "lift up on high the Name of Jesus."

61

The Road to Joy

Song: *I've Discovered the Way of Gladness*
Scripture: Luke 15:1–10
I say unto you, that likewise joy shall be in heaven over one sinner that repenteth, more than over ninety and nine just persons, which need no repentance.

In thousands of homes on Sunday morning a group of clean-cut young people appear on the television screen, singing a beautiful theme song, "I've Discovered the Way of Gladness." Their song comes from Cypress Gardens, and the name of the program is "Day of Discovery." This song, written by Floyd W. Hawkins, was born out of a dark period of religious indecision and spiritual discouragement, as he explains here:

As a teenager I was pretty well out of the church and wayward. Then, in an evangelistic service, I went forward and for the first time realized that faith was accepting God's Word at face value and doing and believing exactly what God said was actually the truth. When that dawned on me, I was so overwhelmed. It was then, at twenty-four years of age, that I started writing songs. For years most of my songs were songs of Christian experience.

186

One of the first ones that I wrote was "He Is No Stranger to Me." "I've Discovered the Way of Gladness" was also one of the songs written because of my awareness of Christ and this new meaning of personal experience. I had learned that Christianity was not a long-faced religion but a way of joy and gladness, and I put it down on paper and we began to sing it. Almost immediately, it began to catch on across the country and people started to sing it. Radio stations were playing it, churches were using it as their theme song and for special meetings. This all happened in 1937.

Floyd Hawkins was born in Pullman, Washington, in 1904, but he did not start his songwriting until he was twenty years of age. The first of his songs to receive any amount of recognition was "Willing to Take the Cross," published by the Rodeheaver Company in 1932. In all he has written almost five hundred songs, few more beautiful than this one:

> Mankind is searching every day,
> In quest of something new,
> But I have found the "living way,"
> The path of pleasures true.
> I've found the Pearl of greatest price,
> "Eternal life" so fair,
> 'Twas through the Savior's sacrifice,
> I found this jewel rare.

> I've discovered the way of gladness,
> I've discovered the way of joy,
> I've discovered relief from sadness,
> 'Tis a happiness without alloy;
> I've discovered the fount of blessing,
> I've discovered the "Living Word."
> 'Twas the greatest of all discoveries,
> When I found Jesus my Lord.

Perhaps you, too, just like Floyd Hawkins, have gone through times of spiritual discouragement, times when you didn't know for sure that you belonged to the Savior or that you were walking beside him as you wanted to. That is when you must find comfort and salvation in God's Word. Take up the Bible as Truth, as young Hawkins did! When you receive salvation and full assurance in the pages of the Scriptures, you can sing with him of the way of gladness you have discovered anew.

Reflection: God's Word can turn our fears into faith, our doubts into doing, our failures into fulfillment, our cowardice into confidence, and our slothfulness into soulwinning.

62

Thoughts of Heaven
Bring a Song

Song: *Shall We Gather at the River?*

Scripture: Revelation 22:1–14

And he shewed me a pure river of water of life, clear as crystal, proceeding out of the throne of God and of the Lamb.

On a hot, sultry day in July 1864, Robert Lowry, a Baptist minister, threw himself on a lounge in his home in a state of exhaustion. He fell to thinking of future things, of the gathering of the saints around God's throne. Then he began to wonder why so many of the hymnwriters had written so much of the "river of death" and so little of the "river of life." A hymn began to take form, first as a question, "Shall we gather at the river?" Then came the answer, "Yes, we'll gather at the river." Soon the words and music to this famous hymn were completed. Now it is a favorite everywhere.

In this day of hurry-scurry and rushing to and fro, more and more people are looking for a place of quiet, peaceful rest. There is nothing on earth more restful than the banks of a winding river. Perhaps this is why God placed a river in heaven, a beautiful crystal river that will make glad the hearts

189

of all God's children when they get to their eternal home. It is
of that "water of life" that Robert Lowry wrote:

> Shall we gather at the river,
> Where bright angel feet have trod;
> With its crystal tide forever,
> Flowing by the throne of God?
>
> *Chorus*:
> Yes, we'll gather at the river,
> The beautiful, the beautiful river,
> Gather with the saints at the river
> That flows by the throne of God.
>
> Soon we'll reach the shining river,
> Soon our pilgrimage will cease,
> Soon our happy hearts will quiver
> With the melody of peace.

Reflection: How comforting it is that heaven is referred to
as a place of rest. After a Christian dies, people often say, "He
was laid to rest." But I'm sure those who have gone on to
heaven are not just lying around resting all of the time! There
are many things to do, both here on earth and in eternity, but
because man is always looking for a place to rest, it makes the
prospect of heaven seem even more precious.

63

Three Days to Live

Song: *Now I Belong to Jesus*
Scripture: Matthew 26:17–30
And when they had sung an hymn, they went out into the mount of Olives.

"How about going with me to the Spanish Town Prison?" a friend asked Roy Gustatson when he was in Jamaica, British West Indies. "We have permission to speak to the prisoners this afternoon."

Gustatson relates the rest of that story:

We met according to appointment, and, after jogging along in a little English Austin, arrived at the prison, where one thousand or more men were incarcerated. The prisoners filed into the large building, similar to a warehouse. Most of them sat on the floor, some on crude benches. After setting up our public address system I sang, played the cornet, and then preached the gospel.

As the men were returning to their cells, a guard stepped up and asked me if I would like to talk to the fourteen men who were condemned to die on the gallows. This was a great surprise, because when a man is doomed to die in Jamaica, not even his wife or mother is allowed to see him. But the guard had permission and led me into the section where three of the fourteen were imprisoned.

It was time to start, but I didn't know how! I realized that I was looking into the faces of men who would never again hear the gospel. This would be their last chance to hear that Jesus Christ offered them eternal life.

Slowly I reached into my case, took my song book out and began to sing Norman Clayton's beautiful song, "Now I Belong to Jesus." I then gave a word of personal testimony, telling how I had turned my life over to God when I was eighteen.

Crouched in his cell before me, looking more like a wild beast than a man, was a fifty-two-year-old murderer. He squinted and said, "I'm going to die on Tuesday morning, sir. Can I be saved? I can't read," he added pathetically. So I read from the Bible verses that show that salvation is God's work and not man's. I'll never forget that experience. He put his face right on that dirty floor and sobbed and cried as he called upon the name of the Lord. After a moment or so, he turned and, smiling through his tears, said, "Sing it again!" "Sing what?" I asked. "What you just sang." So I started to sing once more:

> Now I belong to Jesus,
> Jesus belongs to me.
> Not for the years of time alone,
> But for eternity.

He started to sing it with me, but when we reached the third line he paused. He didn't have "years of time," but only three days.

I left him with my friend, who gave him some further words of assurance as I went to visit an eighteen-year-old murderer, who also confessed Christ that afternoon. When I came back, the three of us stood and sang the song again.

It was time to go. As the guard led us to the huge gate and turned the key, we looked back. There he was, arms waving out through the bars, still singing, "Now I Belong to Jesus." That was the last we saw of him. We heard that on Tuesday morning he went bravely to the gallows, singing as he was ushered into the presence of Christ. They didn't tell us what he was singing, but I think I know.

Do you have the assurance of belonging to Jesus? If not, do what this condemned man did. Ask God to forgive your sins, for "there is no man that sinneth not" (1 Kings 8:46). Accept his remedy: "As many as received him [Jesus Christ], to them gave he power to become the sons of God, even to them that believe on his name" (John 1:12).

Norman Clayton, the composer of this famous song, was born of devout Christian parents who started his Christian training very early. Young Norman started learning to play the piano at age six, and by the time he was twelve had taught himself to play the organ well enough to play for his church.

He has written songs for nearly fifty years, having had more than 750 published. May God bless Norman Clayton for giving to the world this song:

> Jesus, my Lord, will love me forever,
> From Him no pow'r of evil can sever;
> His precious blood He gave to redeem,
> Now I belong to Him.

> *Chorus*
> Now I belong to Jesus,
> Jesus belongs to me.
> Not for the years of time alone,
> But for eternity.

Reflection: Nothing helps the spirit in a time of deep distress more than prayerful singing. Just before Jesus went to suffer, like no other has ever suffered or ever will, he sang with his twelve apostles in the Upper Room, though he knew that his life on earth would soon be the price of redeeming our souls.

64

What Better Inspiration?

Song: *My Jesus, I Love Thee*

Scripture: John 14:23–31

If a man love me, he will keep my words: and my Father will love him, and we will come unto him, and make our abode with him.

Occasionally, in the search for information concerning the story behind a particular hymn, great barriers are encountered. Such is the case with one of our best-loved hymns, "My Jesus, I Love Thee." It was not until recent years that the partial identity of the songwriter, William Ralph Featherstone (1842–78), became known.

It is reported that he probably grew up in Canada, since it was in Toronto in 1858 that he became a Christian. His conversion must have been very special because, just afterward and in connection with this glorious event, he wrote the hymn that is still meaningful to so many people.

The life of every Christian is changed after conversion. The Bible states that then "old things are passed away; behold, all things are become new" (2 Cor. 5:17). Perhaps this young man had been guilty of sins before the Lord Jesus became particu-

194

larly near and dear to him, so he sensed a tremendous need for forgiveness. And we know that those who are forgiven more, love more.

The London Hymn Book first published the song in 1864. By way of this publication, it came to the attention of Dr. A. J. Gordon, a well-known preacher and pastor, who provided the musical setting that has helped make these lines so famous:

> My Jesus, I love Thee, I know Thou art mine;
> For Thee all the follies of sin I resign;
> My gracious Redeemer, my Savior art Thou;
> If ever I loved Thee, my Jesus 'tis now.

As you look back on your life and see the things from which you have been forgiven, there should be a strong tendency to draw closer and increase your love for the Savior.

Reflection: If we will love him, then we must love others. If we pray according to his will, our prayer must be for others. We cannot love him without loving others. "The desire to be loved is ever restless and unsatisfied; but the love that flows out upon others is a perpetual well-spring from on high" (L. M. Child).

65

Making the Choice

Song: *I'd Rather Have Jesus*

Scripture: James 2:1–12

Hearken, my beloved brethren, Hath not God chosen the poor of this world rich in faith, and heirs of the kingdom which he hath promised to them that love him?

"America's beloved gospel singer" is a title given more often to George Beverly Shea than to any other contemporary singer. His rich bass voice, coupled with his sincere Christian attitude, has carried him to the zenith of man's acclaim for gospel soloists. Shea has been associated with evangelist Billy Graham almost since Graham came into national fame through his crusades.

George Beverly Shea yielded his talents and his life to the service of Christ at a very early age, and God has rewarded his faithfulness. Because he realized that in this life only what is done for Christ is of any lasting value, his singing has been a blessing to millions around the world.

"I wrote 'I'd Rather Have Jesus' in 1933," said Shea. "As I sat one evening playing the piano, my mother brought to me a piece of paper on which was written a poem by Rhea Miller.

She thought it to be a very wonderful poem and wanted me to read it. She then asked me to try my hand at writing a melody for it. I began to play as a melody came to me. I then sang and played for the first time 'I'd Rather Have Jesus.'"

In earlier years, Shea had had his share of the lucrative offers of this world, but he thoughtfully turned them down to become a singing servant for the Savior. This world would be a sad place indeed if some men and women could not see beyond the glitter and gloss and choose the more lasting values.

When the rich voice of George Beverly Shea is but a memory, many happy Christians will still be singing his song:

> I'd rather have Jesus than silver or gold,
> I'd rather be His than have riches untold;
> I'd rather have Jesus than houses or lands,
> I'd rather be led by His nail-pierced hand.
>
> I'd rather have Jesus than men's applause,
> I'd rather be faithful to His dear cause;
> I'd rather have Jesus than world-wide fame,
> I'd rather be true to His holy name.
>
> He's fairer than lilies of rarest bloom,
> He's sweeter than honey from out of the comb;
> He's all that my hungering spirit needs.
> I'd rather have Jesus and let Him lead.
>
> *Chorus*:
> Than to be the king of a vast domain
> Or be held in sin's dread sway;
> I'd rather have Jesus than anything
> This world affords today.

Reflection: To have worldly wealth that defies description — and not have Christ — is "vanity of vanities." Yet a real Christian in the throes of abject poverty is rich indeed. It is reported that a child once said, "The Lord is my shepherd. That's all I want."

66

Not Ready to Go In

Song: *Sweet, Sweet Spirit*

Scripture: James 5:7–16

The effectual fervent prayer of a righteous man availeth much.

One Sunday morning, Doris Akers, choir director of the Skypilot Church in Los Angeles, said to her choir, "You are not ready to go in." She didn't believe they had prayed enough! They were accustomed to spending time with her in prayer before the service, asking God to bless their songs. She had once said, "I feel that prayer is more important than great voices." They had already prayed, but this particular morning she asked them to pray again, and they did so with renewed fervor.

As they continued to pray, Doris began to wonder how she could stop this wonderful prayer meeting. She even sent word to the pastor about what was happening. Finally she was compelled to say to the choir, "We have to go. I hate to leave this room and I know you hate to leave, but you know we do have to go to the service. But there is such a sweet, sweet Spirit in this place."

Thus was a new song born. Doris herself explains:

> Songwriters always have their ears open to a song. The song started "singing" to me. I wanted to write it down, but couldn't. I thought the song would be gone after the service. Following the dismissal I went home.
>
> The next morning, to my surprise, I heard the song again, so I went to the piano and wrote:

> > There's a sweet, sweet Spirit in this place,
> > And I know that it's the Spirit of the Lord.
> > There are sweet expressions on each face,
> > And I know they feel the presence of the Lord.
> >
> > Sweet Holy Spirit, sweet Heavenly Dove,
> > Stay right here with us,
> > Filling us with Your love.
> > And for these blessings
> > We lift our hearts in praise;
> > Without a doubt we'll know
> > That we have been revived,
> > When we shall leave this place.

Doris Akers, born in Brookfield, Missouri, was one of ten children. She started writing songs at age ten and has written more than three hundred. At the time of this writing, Doris makes her home in Columbus, Ohio. And she still believes that God wants his children to pray!

Reflection: Not very much worthwhile was ever accomplished apart from prayer. How long has it been since *you* talked with the Lord?

67

He Finally
Heard the Message

Song: *Lord, I'm Coming Home*
Scripture: Luke 15:11–24
I will arise and go to my father, and will say unto him,
Father, I have sinned against heaven, and before thee.

Although we've never heard as much about him as perhaps Fanny Crosby, P. P. Bliss, the Gaithers, or John W. Peterson, he still made a most significant contribution to our singing. He was William J. Kirkpatrick, born in 1838. This man was not only a marvelous lyricist, but his musical settings for poems written by others have afforded us such favorites as "Jesus Saves" and "'Tis So Sweet to Trust in Jesus."

Kirkpatrick was a Methodist choir director and organist, and he especially loved the Methodist camp meetings. During one such meeting, at which he directed the music, he became quite burdened because the invited soloist would sing and then immediately leave, without hearing the sermon or staying to fellowship with other Christians.

After a couple of days of this, Kirkpatrick prayed fervently that God would somehow reach this young man with the gospel of Christ. You see, he feared that the singer had never really known Christ as Savior. As a result, God gave a beautiful song to William Kirkpatrick, which he asked the soloist to sing during an evening service of the meetings. He did so, and he was so convicted in his heart as he sang the words that he decided to stay and hear the sermon. Following the sermon, the singer knelt in the altar area and was gloriously converted.

During that notable camp meeting, near Philadelphia, Pennsylvania, the song that so moved the heart of the soloist and has been used of the Lord to do the same in thousands of hearts ever since was:

> I've wandered far away from God,
> Now I'm coming home;
> The paths of sin too long I've trod —
> Lord, I'm coming home.
>
> Coming home, coming home,
> Nevermore to roam;
> Open now Thine arms of love —
> Lord, I'm coming home.

Nineteen years later, at age eighty-three, Kirkpatrick was sitting up late, working on a music composition. His wife awakened and noticed that the lights were still on in his study. After calling out to him and hearing no response, she went quickly to his study and found him slumped over his last musical offering. He had gone peacefully home to his Lord.

Reflection: "Home" — there is no more beautiful word in the English language to a lonely, lost person. What a glorious prospect — coming home to the arms of the Lord!

68

Freedom's Holy Light

Song: *America (My Country, 'Tis of Thee)*

Scripture: John 8:31–36

If the Son therefore shall make you free, ye shall be free indeed.

What a thrill when Samuel Francis Smith stood in Boston on July 4, 1832, and heard a children's choir at the Park Street Church sing a song he had written.

Five months earlier, Smith, a student at Andover Theological Seminary, had been sitting in his room on the campus that was not very far from the church in which the lantern was hung during Paul Revere's famous ride. Lowell Mason, a music publisher, had given young Smith, who spoke several languages, a number of European music books, thinking that he might translate some of the songs for a new hymnal. Smith's eyes fell on a German song entitled "God Bless Our Native Land." The tune had already been used in England for more than a hundred years as "God Save the King."

Instead of translating the original song, Samuel decided to write new words for the tune. Just thirty minutes before sundown, he picked up a small piece of paper and, as the sun was setting, wrote the last line of what was to become one of the most famous of our country's songs. He later declared that he had not intentionally tried to write a patriotic song, but it soon became so popular that it almost became our national anthem.

Later, Samuel Francis Smith became a Baptist preacher and went on to author several books, teach languages at Newton Center, hold a number of positions with his denomination, and write one hundred and fifty hymns. His most famous hymn is a missionary song, "The Morning Light Is Breaking."

During his eighty-eighth year, Smith passed away at a train station as he was about to board. He had a long and useful life, was a blessing and inspiration to many, and left you and me:

> My country, 'tis of thee,
> Sweet land of liberty,
> Of thee I sing:
> Land where my fathers died,
> Land of the pilgrims' pride,
> From every mountainside
> Let freedom ring!
>
> Our fathers' God, to Thee,
> Author of liberty,
> To Thee we sing:
> Long may our land be bright
> With freedom's holy light;
> Protect us by Thy might,
> Great God, our King!

Reflection: One of the foremost blessings you and I enjoy from God's hand is the freedom to live in America, "sweet land of liberty." Yet, our most cherished freedom is available to all God's children: the liberation from the bondage of sin.

69

The Little Lake Song

Song: *A Perfect Heart*

Scripture: Psalm 62

Also unto thee, O Lord, belongeth mercy: for thou renderest to every man according to his work.

What a thrill for Dony and Reba Rambo McGuire to arrive at a large gathering in Zimbabwe, Africa, and hear thousands of happy Christians singing one of their beautiful songs, first in their native language and then in an attempt at English. Reba reports, "I was so moved that I was reduced to an emotional basket case for a few moments." That song, "A Perfect Heart," was born several years before on Center Hill Lake, near Nashville, Tennessee.

Reba, an only child, was born October 17, 1951, in Madisonville, Kentucky, to Buck and Dottie Rambo and began her musical career very early. She relates that "from my earliest recollection there were guitars, pianos, mandolins and banjos around. Music has been a constant with me during my whole life. I began traveling with my parents at age thirteen and have been traveling ever since." She and her husband, Dony, now bring their ministry of music to thousands in many churches and auditoriums.

Dony was born in Tulsa, Oklahoma, in 1951, one of seven children. He studied music for many years, in high school, college, and beyond. Beginning his songwriting in 1975, he has written both on his own and in association with such notables as Gloria Gaither and his wife. Dony was an accomplished pianist, songwriter, and recording artist before his marriage to Reba in 1980.

The story behind "A Perfect Heart" began when friends invited the McGuires to vacation with them on their houseboat on a lake near Nashville. They had determined to work diligently on their songwriting during that time, and they did so. They prayed earnestly that the Lord would do something special through them that week. At the end of the week they had completed a number of songs and done some work on a musical. Reba finishes the story in her own words:

> On the very last morning we were to be on the boat, Dony got up very early to try to catch a catfish for breakfast. He is an early riser. I was so full of faith in his fishing ability that I proceeded to the kitchen and started to cook bacon and eggs.
>
> The sun was peeking over the hills and a mist was rising from the water. It was a glorious morning. I looked out of a small porthole and caught a glimpse of Dony with a strange look on his face. Some people come down with a cold, while Dony comes down with a song! I couldn't explain it, but I knew something good was about to happen. I turned off the burners where I was cooking and removed the food. I gathered our songwriting materials and sat down to wait for him to come in.
>
> When he came in a few minutes later, he sat down before a small electric piano and began to play. As he played what the Lord was giving to him, I began to write lyrics as they were being given to me. That kind of inspiration had only occurred a few times in our short songwriting career together. It was as if God was saying, "You've been faithful in your praying and studying for a week; now, I'm going to give you something, just because I have the power to do so." I wrote as fast as I could

write, while Dony continued to play. We both completed the whole composition and have never changed a word or the musical setting.

It became our "little lake song." We used it for a time around our offices as a devotional song and sang it at a few small churches.

One day Bill Gaither came by our offices and heard us singing it during one of our devotional periods. He asked where we got it. We told him it was our "lake song." He expressed such a keen interest in it that Dony made a tape of it for him. That started it on its way.

And so, several years later, halfway around the world in Zimbabwe, the McGuires heard their "little lake song" being sung by the great host of Africans gathered there. They were singing:

> Morning sun, light of creation;
> Grassy fields, a velvet floor;
> Silver clouds, a shimmering curtain;
> He's designed a perfect world.
>
> I'm amazed at His talents,
> Stand in awe of One so great;
> Now my soul begins to sing out
> To the source from which it came.
>
> Bless the Lord who reigns in beauty;
> Bless the Lord who reigns with wisdom and with pow'r.
> Bless the Lord who fills my life with so much love,
> He can make a perfect heart.

Dony and Reba make their home in the Atlanta area. They continue to travel, crisscrossing our country, singing and writing songs.

Reflection: The Lord will always reward your faithful attention to his leading. It may not be with a song, but it will be with his choice of some good work you can do for him.

70

The Bells Toll,
and a Song Is Born

Song: *Ring the Bells*

Scripture: Psalm 48

*According to thy name, O God, so is thy praise unto the ends
of the earth: thy right hand is full of righteousness.*

In 1950, Harry and Millie Bollback boarded a ship
bound for South America. He was to spend the next twenty
years as a missionary in Brazil, the first five of which would be
in the jungles of the Amazon, working among the Xavanti
Indians. Harry thought he was sailing away from a career in
music, perhaps never to play seriously again, although he had
wanted to be a concert pianist.

By age sixteen Harry Bollback had already played in concerts and in Christian crusades with audiences numbering into
the tens of thousands. Little did he realize at the time that he
would rear his family in Brazil, that he would suffer perils in
the jungles of the Amazon, and that he would come close to
death at the hands of the Xavanti Indians. Many times he
would have to rely on the promises of God and trust him

explicitly for provision, safety, and the wisdom to handle the unusual situations in which he would find himself.

Harry was born in Brooklyn, New York, on January 20, 1925. Since early childhood he loved music. His dad and his Sunday school teacher in the Faith Gospel Mission taught him to play the piano. He took it very seriously, and his practicing paid off. He played his first concert at age twelve.

Life took a drastic right turn for Harry at age sixteen. He found himself at a Christian camp, not having a particularly great time. In fact, he was so unruly that the persons in charge decided to send him home, but they were waiting until morning. That night he was wonderfully converted to Christ as Lord and Savior.

Shortly thereafter Harry met Jack Wyrtzen, the founder of Word of Life. Bollback has been associated with that organization until the present. During the earlier years of his ministry, as pianist at Word of Life, he was given time off to continue his music studies at Philadelphia School of the Bible. A few years later he felt the call of God to Brazil.

After seven years in that needy place, he decided one day to visit a friend in a nearby town. During this historic visit one of our greatest Christmas songs was written. Following is the story as Harry Bollback told it:

> I was waiting in a long line at the bus station in Sao Paulo, waiting for a bus to take me to visit a fellow missionary, Paul Overholt. It was Christmas time. The city was beautifully decorated. It was about six o'clock and bells were ringing everywhere, for "the hour of Mary." The people all seemed so excited. In this Catholic country, where Mary is so adored and worshipped, my thoughts turned to the birth of Christ. Like a dayspring, words and music began to pour into my mind. I quickly found a piece of paper and wrote the whole song down as it came to me—still standing in line.
>
> I could hardly wait to get to my friend's house, so I could hear how it would sound. Paul was a singer, working with Youth For Christ in that country, and I wanted to hear him sing it.
>
> When I reached Paul's house, I sat down at the piano and

played it. Paul was really excited about it and was the first person to sing it. I had nothing to do with the writing of it. The Lord just gave it.

Ring the bells! ring the bells! Let the whole world know
Christ was born in Bethlehem, many years ago;
Born to die that man might live; came to earth new life to give,
Born of Mary, born so low, many years ago.

God the Father gave His Son; gave His own Beloved One
To this wicked, sinful earth, to bring mankind His love — new
   birth!
Ring the bells! ring the bells! Let the whole world know
Christ was born in Bethlehem many years ago.

Ring the bells! ring the bells! Let the whole world know.
Christ the Savior lives today; as He did so long ago!

"Ring the Bells" was later published by Zondervan Publishing Company and sold more than one million copies in sheet-music form. Countless numbers have come to know Christ as a direct result of the writing of that song. Bollback later wrote a musical of the same title, with the song as its base. Hundreds of thousands of people have been blessed by hearing it performed in many places in our country.

Reflection: Each year at Christmas time, as you hear the tolling of the bells, be reminded that the world still needs to know the Christ who was born in Bethlehem, many years ago.

71

His Greatest Achievement

Song: *First Place*

Scripture: Colossians 1:1–18

And he is the head of the body, the church: who is the beginning, the firstborn from the dead; that in all things he might have the pre-eminence.

One of the most influential figures in youth music for many years has been Thurlow Spurr. He was born January 1, 1934, in Broadalbin, New York, into the home of a pastor and missionary to children. Thurlow, his brother and sister, and their parents formed a family musical group that sang and played a number of instruments. According to Spurr, it was a foretaste of things to come.

As a student at Bob Jones University, Thurlow directed a student musical group called Missions on the March. This, too, helped prepare him for a later ministry among young people in the Youth for Christ movement.

While minister of music at Salem Baptist Church in Winston-Salem, North Carolina, in the early sixties, he formed a small ensemble of eight voices. At first he called them The Choralaires. While sitting in church one evening, the pastor,

Dr. Charles Stevens, as he had often done in the past, inadvertently referred to Thurlow as "Spurrlow Thurr." One of the group leaned over to Thurlow and said, "Why don't we call our group The Spurrlows?" The name stuck, and the group traveled the length and breadth of this country as Thurlow Spurr and The Spurrlows.

The musical group grew larger, at one time reaching a total of twenty-eight. They sang in churches, city auditoriums, and high school assemblies. For a time they were sponsored by the Chrysler Corporation.

Thurlow was not given to being a prolific songwriter, but on one occasion he reached great heights. Here is his story as he told it:

> My wife and I were traveling on the turnpike, making our way from Chicago to Philadelphia, during the Easter season in 1960. As we traveled through Ohio it began to get dark. I'm a "let's go one more exit" kind of a person. I like to get as far as possible before stopping. But we were tired and decided to stop for the night. I had forgotten that many people travel on that weekend. They were doing as we were—looking for a place to stay.
>
> At one exit there were five or six large motels, but no place for us. We continued on the turnpike and did the same thing at several other exits. Finally I asked my wife to drive. I began to think, "How many of these people who are crowding the highways and jamming these hotels have any time or place for the Lord in their lives? Do they really understand that this is a celebration of the time when Jesus was triumphant over the grave and death?"
>
> As those thoughts kept passing through my mind, I reached for a piece of paper and began to write, trying to keep up with the ideas that flooded my mind. My cry, as I wrote the words, was that people would give Christ first place, if they gave him any place at all. And so I, with the light on in the car, unceremoniously wrote:
>
> Are you longing for someone to guide you each day—
> Someone who knows every step of the way?

When you're wondering why there are clouds in your sky,
I have the answer for you. . . .

Why don't you give Him a place in your heart?
Don't turn away; from His love depart.
You'll find happiness right from the start
As you give Him first place in your heart.

This song went on to be used in youth crusades and conventions all over America. In the large conventions it was used as an invitation song and has blessed thousands as they welcomed Jesus Christ in their hearts.

Reflection: At Easter, Christmas, Thanksgiving or any other time of the year, the Lord should have "First Place" in our lives.

72

Not a Sermon, a Song!

Song: *Yesterday, Today, and Tomorrow*
Scripture: Hebrews 13:1–9
Jesus Christ the same yesterday, and to day and for ever.

Fortunate indeed was Don Wyrtzen to grow up at a place like Word of Life in Schroon Lake, New York. His father, Dr. Jack Wyrtzen, was the founder of this worldwide ministry and has directed its activities for several decades.

Born August 16, 1942, Don states that he was interested in music as far back as he can remember. He developed an insatiable desire to be an arranger of choir music—a flame fueled by his association with a number of notable composers and arrangers who were guests at Word of Life, a Christian retreat and campground.

During his growing-up years, Don attended Maplewood Gospel Chapel, a Plymouth Brethren Assembly church. Since then he has been active in a number of other churches. He is presently a member of the Brentwood Baptist Church near Nashville, Tennessee.

Following his college and seminary days at Moody Bible

Institute, The King's College, and Dallas Theological Seminary, Don joined the staff of Singspiration Music in Grand Rapids, Michigan. During his music-writing years, he has written more than two hundred anthems and gospel songs. His choral collections and musicals have sold approximately two million copies, but his songwriting is, in his words, "a fringe benefit" to his arranging.

Each summer, during his college days, Don worked in the music program at Word of Life, which had a radio program on the American Broadcasting Company network and a television ministry. In the fall of 1965, just after Don entered seminary, he called his dad and asked if he had any ideas for songs. He was helping put together another book of songs and choruses for the sessions at Schroon Lake the following summer. The elder Wyrtzen said, "No, but I have a very good sermon outline." He continued, "You know, there are only three days in the life of a Christian. *Yesterday*—he died for us. That's Calvary. *Today*—he lives for us. He ever lives in heaven to manage all of our concerns here on earth. *Tomorrow*—he comes for us. So there are three days: yesterday, today, and tomorrow."

Young Wyrtzen jotted down those thoughts. His father was wondering whether he should preach on the subject. But the next thing he knew, his son had sent him a new song from the idea that he had received:

> Yesterday He died for me, yesterday, yesterday,
> Yesterday He died for me, yesterday.
> Yesterday He died for me, died for me—
> This is history.
>
> Today He lives for me, today, today,
> Today He lives for me, today.
> Today He lives for me, lives for me—
> This is victory.
>
> Tomorrow He comes for me, He comes, He comes.
> Tomorrow He comes for me, He comes.
> Tomorrow He comes for me, comes for me—
> This is mystery.

O friend, do you know Him? know Him? know Him?
O friend, do you know Him? know Him?
O friend, do you know Him, do you know Him?
Jesus Christ, the Lord, Jesus Christ, the Lord,
Jesus Christ, the Lord.

That song has gone over most of the world and has been sung in other languages. What a marvelous message "Yesterday, Today and Tomorrow" contains!

Reflection: What a wonderful Guide and Keeper our Savior is to us. He has gone before us. He now walks beside us. And he can see the pathway ahead and knows exactly where it leads—to a glorious tomorrow!

73

The Band Was
Not Yet for Them

Song: *Finally Home*

Scripture: Acts 7:52–60

But he, being full of the Holy Ghost, looked up stedfastly into heaven, and saw the glory of God, and Jesus standing on the right hand of God, And said, Behold, I see the heavens opened, and the Son of man standing on the right hand of God.

Dr. W. A. Criswell, pastor of the famed First Baptist Church in Dallas, Texas, tells the following story:

A missionary and his wife, broken in health after spending a lifetime in Africa, were on a large ship making their way back home, to the United States. They were anxious to see the homeland once again.

Among the passengers on this particular trip was President Theodore Roosevelt, returning from a safari in Africa, a big-game hunting expedition. The missionary turned to his wife and said, "I wonder, will anyone be there to meet us when we arrive?" As they neared the port they could see a large throng waving and shouting. A band was playing. It was evident that the President was to have a great reception. But, as the missionaries stepped on shore and looked about, not a single person was there to greet them or to welcome them home.

That night, in a cheap hotel room, the old missionary began to reflect on the happenings of the day and the lack of a reception for them. He said to his wife, "The President can go to Africa to kill some animals, and when he returns great crowds come out to greet him and welcome him back. We have given our lives in Africa, telling people about Christ, leading them to life in him, and when *we* return there is not one soul to greet us." She could sense his deep disappointment and agony of soul. Finally, in desperation, she said, "I don't know how to help you. I'm going to leave you alone for a while and I want you to talk to God about it."

After she left, he fell to his knees and poured out his heart to the Lord. He told God, "I can't understand and I don't know why this would happen to me." After a few moments, the Lord seemed to calm his heart and to assure him that he was not finally home, yet. He would get his big reception in heaven.

After telling this story, Dr. Criswell closed with: "Just think of stepping on shore and finding it heaven, of touching a hand and finding it God's, of breathing new air and finding it celestial, of waking up in Glory and finding it home."

Don Wyrtzen, then a young student at Dallas Theological Seminary, was asked by Dr. Criswell's daughter, Ann, to put her dad's closing remarks to music. He did so, in just about ten minutes, and promptly forgot all about it.

Following his seminary days, young Wyrtzen, in the spring of 1971, went to work for Singspiration music company. The song he had begun earlier was introduced at a choral seminar in Boca Raton, Florida, sponsored by Singspiration. It happened because Ann Criswell was a special soloist for the seminar and wanted to use Wyrtzen's chorus. They decided to tack it onto another song, "O That Will Be Glory for Me." The well-known composer John W. Peterson heard the medley and was greatly impressed with the effectiveness of the short chorus. He suggested to Wyrtzen that he write verses to go with it, contrasting the life on this earth, which is often difficult, with the life that awaits every Christian in heaven. In just a few days he had the verses completed.

The song has become a favorite in many circles. It has often been used as a triumphant background for celebrating the homegoing of a victorious Christian. In the opinion of this writer, the song will become a part of Christian hymnody that will endure for generations.

Don Wyrtzen continues to write gospel songs and anthems, arrange choral music (his first love) and to orchestrate and produce Christian recordings. The Lord may give him a long life and allow him to do many things, but Christians everywhere will always be thankful to him and to Dr. Criswell for letting the Lord use them to give to us this victorious song, "Finally Home!"

> When engulfed by the terror of tempestuous sea,
> Unknown waves before you roll;
> At the end of doubt and peril is eternity,
> Though fear and conflict seize your soul:
>
> *Chorus*:
> But just think of stepping on shore
> And finding it Heaven!
> Of touching a hand and finding it God's!
> Of breathing new air and finding it celestial!
> Of waking up in Glory and finding it home!
>
> When surrounded by the blackness of the darkest night,
> O how lonely death can be;
> At the end of this long tunnel is a shining light,
> For death is swallowed up in victory!

Reflection: Only in our imaginations can we now enjoy the blessings of the marvelous, glorious reality that awaits every Christian.